"This book is a comprehensive, practical, clearly written explanation of the concept and its relationship to quality, vendors, and manufacturing technology. Examples from actual companies illustrate the managerial problems involved in changing to JIT. In a nutshell, this book tells you why the JIT approach makes sense, cautions on its implications, and then tells you how to go about it."

JEFFREY G. MILLER
Professor, Operations Management
Director, Manufacturing Roundtable
School of Management
Boston University

"Finally . . . a book on JIT that says everything.
Ed Hay started us on the JIT journey three years ago and we can attest to his why and how-to approach to implementation. He clarifies JIT objectives, systematically outlines the process of getting started and cautions on the pitfalls, converting a deceptively confusing concept into a successful and rewarding experience."

JOSEPH F. REARDON
Plant Manager
Schrader Bellows

"This is a dynamic book. Ed Hay has the uncanny ability to get down to basics of Just In Time, which is simplicity. The book supports the basic premises of JIT through easy-to-understand, real life examples."

PETER LANDRY
Xerox Corporation

". . . Ed Hay has captured the essence of the JIT philosophy with a perspective of an experienced practitioner. We at Miliken find his approach to eliminate the "non-value adding" product flow steps to be especially practical."

ROGER MILIKEN
Chairman and Chief Executive Officer
Miliken & Company

THE JUST-IN-TIME BREAKTHROUGH

Implementing the New Manufacturing Basics

EDWARD J. HAY

Rath and Strong, Inc.

JOHN WILEY & SONS

New York · Chichester · Brisbane · Toronto · Singapore

Library of Congress Cataloging-in-Publication Data:

Hay, Edward J.

The just-in-time breakthrough.

Bibliography: p.
Includes index.
1. Production control. 2. Inventory control.
I. Title.

TS157.H38   1988   658.5   87-25315
ISBN 0-471-85413-1

Printed in the United States of America

10 9 8 7 6 5 4

ACKNOWLEDGEMENTS

As are most things at Rath & Strong, this book was a team effort. I want to thank Dan Ciampa for getting the whole process started when he made it his personal goal to help me find a way to make this book happen in spite of an already overloaded schedule. Dan also contributed directly to some of the sections on implementation. I would also like to thank Dick Feeney who spent a great deal of time he really didn't have evenings and weekends writing or rewriting some of the technical sections. Thanks also to Romey Everdell who contributed major portions of Chapter 9.

I owe a special note of thanks to Jon Zonderman, the professional writer who did the bulk of the actual writing. I appreciate not only his patience and professionalism through thick and thin, but also the fact that the end result clearly sounds like me. Meredith Allen must also be recognized for her role in coordinating the many steps and activities, both internally and with the publisher, and keeping us pretty much on schedule in spite of ourselves.

On a more basic level, this book would not be possible without the wealth of experience gained from helping many clients implement JIT. It is therefore fitting to acknowledge those individuals most responsible for my becoming a consultant in the first place. First, I thank two gentlemen from my former employer, Fram Corporation (although I didn't thank them at the time), whose adamant refusal to let me implement JIT led to a career change into consulting. Second, I thank Ernest Anderson who at that critical time gave me the help and counsel necessary to give me the courage, after 23 years of getting comfortable in industry, to take the plunge into the unfamiliar territory of consulting. Last, but most important, I thank my wife and partner whose support and encouragement has continued through circumstances most "normal" people would not put up with.

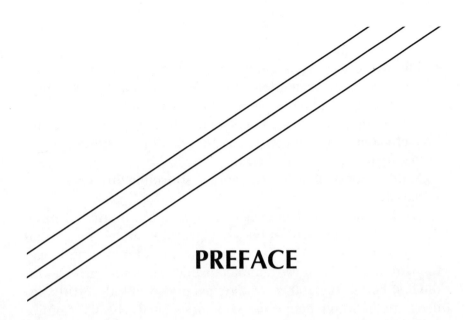

PREFACE

U.S. and other Western manufacturing companies have a limited number of options if they are going to transform themselves into world-class competitors in the 1990s and beyond.

They can work harder at the traditional methods of cost cutting to get a less expensive manufacturing system. But, cost cutting has proved to be not nearly enough to close the competitive gap between Western manufacturers and other countries.

They can increase automation, which requires large capital outlays and brings with it the risks of inflexibility, complexity, and large overheads.

OR they can opt for a revolutionary simplification and streamlining of the existing manufacturing system using the Just-In-Time philosophy of manufacturing and purchasing. Although JIT seems at first blush to be antithetical to traditional Western notions of manufacturing, I believe it is truly the best option for Western companies and an option that should be explored by every company.

And the notion that JIT can work is spreading throughout corporate America and abroad.

Just-In-Time manufacturing—producing the minimum number of units in the smallest possible quantities at the latest possible time and eliminating the reasons for inventory—is no longer thought of as a "Japanese manufacturing technique" as it was for the first half of the 1980s. Yet few people, even today, truly understand the implementation issues associated with JIT. Continually people tell me: "I know all about the JIT philosophy and the theories behind it. My question is, how do I do it in my company?"

The purpose of this book is to show these people how to think through the issues involved in implementing JIT production in their businesses and to assure them that JIT can work for them.

The issues associated with JIT can be seen as falling into two main categories. First, there are technological issues—how to level the load, set up work cells, and reduce machine set-up time. Second, there are numerous management issues—the greatest being how to foster a climate within the corporation under which a successful change to a JIT environment can take place. To do this, senior management must understand the benefits JIT can have to the company, and middle management and direct labor must understand the benefits of JIT to them.

Measurement, reward, and information systems must be redesigned to help a company's personnel break down old ways of thinking and working. They must intellectually "clean house" in order to get everyone off to a fresh start.

Western business people are too often mystified by JIT because of its perceived association with Japan. They fail to break the philosophy into its parts and determine that it is little more than good old-fashioned manufacturing know-how and common sense, much of which first came into being in the United States. One of the first steps toward successfully implementing JIT in the United States and other Western countries is to stop thinking of it as Japanese and think of it as getting back to manufacturing basics.

Since the end of World War II U.S. manufacturers have developed a way of doing business where they plan, replan, and plan some more. Planning, of course, is fine, but unfortunately it has become an end in itself. While we have improved our ability to plan and replan we have neglected our ability to carry out these manufacturing plans. The JIT philosophy stresses getting the manufacturing process under control, then keeping it under control, so that the first plan can be executed without the need for any replanning.

In this and many other ways, JIT is a powerful production-enhancing philosophy, as opposed to merely a cost-cutting tool. For Westerners to let the opportunity to implement it go by would not only be foolish but disastrous.

I have worked with all kinds of companies to implement Just-In-Time manufacturing. JIT has helped client companies recognize the following benefits:

Twenty percent to 50 percent increases in direct and indirect labor productivity

Thirty percent to 40 percent increases in equipment capacity

Eighty percent to 90 percent reductions in manufacturing lead time

Forty percent to 50 percent reductions in the cost of failure (scrap, rework, and warranties)

Eight percent to 15 percent reductions in the cost of purchased material

Fifty percent to 90 percent reductions in inventories

Thirty percent to 40 percent reductions in space requirements.

Although not every company receives every benefit, examples abound of companies making dramatic gains in two, three, or more of these areas in only a few months. And what's best, JIT is a low-cost or no-cost way of achieving these gains.

The road to a harmonious JIT manufacturing and purchasing environment is not often easy. But it is almost always rewarding. By working hard at a relatively small number of simple, common-sense steps, Western manufacturing companies can once again become world class.

EDWARD J. HAY

East Greenwich, Rhode Island
October, 1987

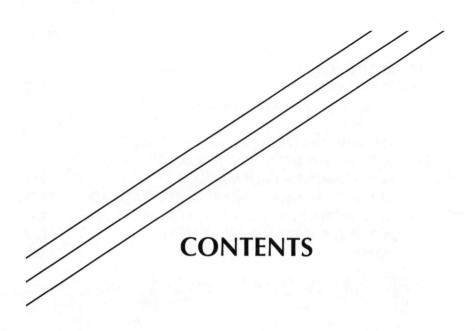

CONTENTS

THE JUST-IN-TIME BREAKTHROUGH

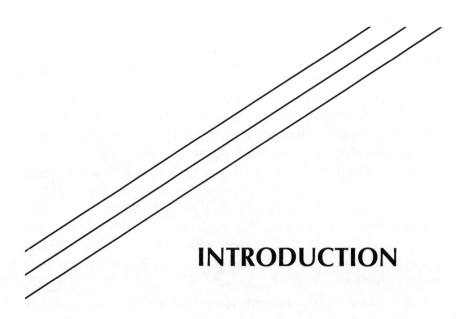

INTRODUCTION

Just In Time. The words have been bandied about since the early 1980s by Western manufacturers. But many people still don't understand exactly what Just In Time is. They think it is a system or a gimmick for reducing inventories, pushing responsibilities onto suppliers, or merely a quick fix for inefficient manufacturing.

In truth, Just In Time is much more.

Just In Time (JIT) is a manufacturing philosophy, a philosophy of eliminating waste in the total manufacturing process, from purchasing through distribution. If this philosophy is properly implemented, JIT enables a company to develop manufacturing into a strategic weapon.

Too often since JIT came to America's shores, companies have used the philosophy only to cut costs and attain greater profits. This is a short-term view of JIT's potential, and will, like all other short-term solutions, eventually falter.

The long-term result of eliminating waste is a manufacturing process that is so streamlined, cost efficient, quality oriented, and responsive to the customer that it becomes a strategic weapon. By having a more efficient, less wasteful manufacturing system, companies will no longer be forced to depend on marketing and advertising as the only ways to differentiate products and capture market share.

Just In Time not only affords companies great increases in quality of their manufactured goods. It allows a company to cut response time to market by as much as 90 percent. New products or product changes requested by the customer can be brought to market in half the time it currently takes. At the same time, the capital equipment necessary to do this can be reduced and inventories can be drastically cut, if not eliminated.

With successful implementation of JIT, companies that in the past have been forced to market themselves as service- and quality-oriented, because they were unable to compete on price, can begin to see themselves as low-cost producers. This could open up completely new markets for the companies, and help differentiate the company from all other service- and quality-oriented companies.

Because JIT offers these opportunities, it is imperative for a company to plan for and implement JIT in conjunction with a total business or marketing plan. Often, because of a company's strategic goals, certain elements of JIT will be important to carry out early while other elements will not be as important. On the other hand, given the opportunities provided by JIT, some companies will want to modify or even rewrite their business or marketing plans to fit better with JIT opportunities.

ELIMINATING WASTE

As part of the JIT philosophy, there are three basic and equally important components for eliminating waste.

The first basic component of waste elimination is establishing balance and synchronization and flow in the manufacturing process, either where it does not exist or where it can be enhanced.

The second component is the company's attitude toward quality, the idea of "doing it right the first time."

The third component of the Just In Time philosophy is employee involvement. It is a prerequisite for waste elimination. Every member of the organization—from the shop floor to senior management—has a part to play in the elimination of waste and solving the manufacturing problems that cause waste. The only way a company can solve the hundreds or even thousands of problems that occur in a manufacturing system—from small problems to large—is total employee involvement.

SUCCESS

I want to tell you a success story, about Hutchinson Technology, Inc., a Rath and Strong client.*

Hutchinson Technology, Inc. had a problem.

In the early 1980s offshore competition—primarily from Japan—was putting pressure on the company to reduce costs of its six product lines. One company went so far as to give Hutchinson an ultimatum—reduce the price of one product by 67 percent in the next 12 to 18 months or else.

Hutchinson is a 20-year-old custom manufacturer of computer

*The specific information in this story was supplied by Wayne Fortun, President of Hutchinson Technology, Inc., Arnold Putnam, Chairman Emeritus, then President of Rath & Strong, Inc. and John Cingari, Principal of Rath & Strong, Inc.

components and complex electronic assemblies. The company employs between 1000 and 1200 people at six manufacturing facilities, all operating under one roof in Hutchinson, Minnesota.

At the same time Hutchinson was faced with its cost-cutting dilemma, the company was trying to generate more revenue with the same number of employees. In short, Hutchinson needed a more efficient operation.

Hutchinson found the solution to its problems in Just-In-Time manufacturing. Hutchinson's move to JIT was initiated by its president, Wayne Fortun, who in 1983 traveled to Japan with a Rath and Strong-sponsored executive group to visit manufacturing companies there and study Japanese manufacturing practices. Fortun was impressed by the JIT operations he saw and wanted to implement JIT techniques at Hutchinson.

"At the time, we were using state-of-the-art production processes that gave us average yields of 55 percent good quality," Fortun recalled. "And I realized that unless our quality levels could be raised significantly, we would have a tough time with JIT."

To lay the groundwork for JIT implementation, Rath and Strong worked with Hutchinson on a quality-improvement program that focused on changing operations on the shop floor. Intended to stabilize Hutchinson's manufacturing process and increase yields, the program included a videotape course on Total Quality, a statistical problem-solving section, and general quality training.

Video courses were presented to eight multidisciplinary task teams representing workers from management to operations level personnel. They were held once a week for 8 to 16 weeks.

The problem-solving sessions were attended by a smaller group, once every three weeks, for a 15-week period. These were complemented with projects in the plant.

Quality training for managers and operators occurred over a period of several months. Overall, the quality improvement program resulted in a 33 percent improvement in quality yields, raising the total to over 70 percent, including many state-of-the-art processes.

Following the success of this program, Hutchinson took its next step toward implementing JIT. In August, 1985, the company invited us to conduct a two-day JIT seminar for Hutchinson employees. The seminar, presented to managers and supervisors, outlined the principles of JIT, described the techniques of JIT operations, and included a discussion of JIT's potential benefits.

In September, Hutchinson created JIT implementation teams in each of its six manufacturing divisions—Complex Assembly, Thin-Film Suspension, Flexible Circuits, Component Manufacturing, Custom Manufacturing, and Cable Assembly.

Each team included the manufacturing manager, a quality representative, a production supervisor, a process engineer, and an industrial engineer. The complex assembly and thin-film suspension groups were the first to begin, immediately implementing pilot machine cells in their areas for a 30-day trial period.

In October, John Cingari, my colleague at Rath and Strong, traveled to Minnesota to help Hutchinson begin to implement JIT in all manufacturing groups. From October through the following July he spent two days each month at the plant, assisting the six JIT implementation teams.

Cingari's efforts were focused on working with Hutchinson to understand and implement four of the five basic JIT techniques—machine cells, pull systems, setup reduction, and uniform plant load.

The Complex Assembly and Cable Assembly groups implemented machine cells, pull systems, and uniform plant load. Thin-Film Suspension and Flexible Circuits implemented machine cells, pull systems, setup reduction, and uniform plant load. Custom and Component Manufacturing implemented pull systems, setup reduction, and uniform plant load.

Specifically, Cingari helped the individual groups identify sites for pilot applications, offered technical training on the five techniques of JIT and their principles, and helped design and review layouts for machine cells in those groups that used them. In the early stages, he taught members of the JIT teams how to get started with the machine cells, and helped manufacturing managers and industrial engineers determine the best way to maximize workers' time and determine crew sizes that could be flexible to constantly changing demand rates.

After three months of successful pilot applications, Hutchinson integrated JIT through all the manufacturing functions, extending the pilots that existed in isolated areas to all functions on the plant floor.

Though the JIT implementation effort was still underway at Hutchinson as of the end of 1986, the company had in just over a year realized dramatic improvements above and beyond those realized during the quality campaign. Specifically:

Manufacturing lead times were reduced from 50 to 90 percent.

Quality yields improved an additional 4 to 14 percent.

Setup times were reduced by as much as 75 percent.

Work-in-process was reduced 40 to 90 percent—that translated into 80 work-in-process inventory turns and 120 inventory turns in finished goods.

These improvements in individual areas of manufacturing are only part of the Hutchinson picture, however. The big story is that at a time when the electronics industry was suffering, JIT helped Hutchinson remain competitive and maintain market share. The company that had issued the ultimatum to Hutchinson a year earlier—drop the price 67 percent or we will have our work done offshore—stayed with Hutchinson and is, in 1987, a major customer.

In addition, Hutchinson was able to respond to competitive pressures on its major product line (more than half of its total business). It maintained market share by lowering its price by 30 percent *while increasing its percent profit on each unit by one third.* And the quality of Hutchinson's product is so good that the company is able to compete in the Far East, shipping some 30 percent of its product to Far East manufacturers.

Clearly, JIT and Quality have been a success at Hutchinson— and in a very short time. Within nine months Hutchinson was operating under JIT, which is dramatically faster than almost any other company we have worked with.

There were two major factors in Hutchinson's success in implementing JIT and making it work. One was all the previous work the company had put into its quality program. The other, equally important factor was top management's dedication to the JIT concept.

"The top management team at Hutchinson is the JIT champion," Cingari said. "From the beginning, top management thought through the idea conceptually and was totally committed to implementing it. And they passed that feeling on to workers at all levels of the company.

"Even before the effort was started, Hutchinson's management team had created a corporate culture for risk-taking and experimentation with new concepts. Each JIT team's charter was not to study JIT, but to experiment with it wherever the team felt it was appropriate. The teams were given the clear message from top management that experimentation was highly regarded. So there was no fear of failure."

Teamwork also played an important role in Hutchinson's success. Teamwork is crucial to successful implementation of JIT and continued successful JIT operation.

While the first year of JIT's implementation and operation at Hutchinson has been a success, the company is not satisfied yet. Following the JIT principle that says companies should strive for continuous improvement, Hutchinson is planning to bring its suppliers into the JIT fold by implementing Just-In-Time purchasing—the fifth JIT technique.

This book will use examples like Hutchinson to present the first full-scale rendering of the Western version of the Just-In-Time manufacturing philosophy. By full-scale I mean that I will not only deal with the technical aspects of JIT, but give equal time and attention to the management issues involved in successfully implementing JIT in Western cultures. Previous books have only dealt with the technical aspects, and usually with a Japanese model.

Throughout this book I will discuss a model of JIT that has worked for Hutchinson and other U.S. companies since the early 1980s for whom I have served as a consultant. This model has worked for U.S., Canadian, and European divisions of these companies as early as 1981. Beginning in 1985, these companies started to implement some of these techniques in their Mexican and South American divisions as well.

Certain issues vary from country to country, or from continent to continent, but many are common across international boundaries throughout the West.

This book, then, has two major functions and two major parts.

One is an explanation of the technical aspects of JIT and how to make those technical aspects work.

The second and more complex part is a discussion of the difficult management issues involved in implementing these technical changes. Some of these implementation difficulties are the changing of attitudes and the company climate with regard to manufacturing, getting the involvement of middle management and individuals on the shop floor, and rethinking the company's measurement and reward systems. These three elements are intimately involved with one another.

Slowly but surely the JIT ideal of manufacturing excellence is filtering through the world. This will lead to heightened competition; but in the long run, it will also lead to prosperity as resources are put into production rather than wasted.

1

BUT WILL IT WORK
IN MY COMPANY?

One of the first questions asked by top executives who are first getting interested in JIT is: "But will it work in my company?" Executives and managers may think there are features unique to their company that force them to work in particular ways. Often they believe the way they operate is unique. But it is usually just a variation on a theme of Western manufacturing, and that theme is dictated by Western and individual corporate cultures, industry tradition and, to a large extent, human nature.

The message to these people and companies is: Just-In-Time manufacturing can work in any manufacturing environment, in any industry. In fact, we are now learning that it can work in nonmanufacturing industries as well.

Simply put, Just In Time is a few basic assumptions, about the right way to manufacture and the right way to conduct business with suppliers and customers, that lead to efficient, productive manufacturing. There is nothing magical about JIT. It ultimately boils down to a few basics executed well.

A LITTLE HISTORY

Just In Time began some time after World War II as the Toyota Production System. Until the late 1970s, the system was limited to Toyota and the Toyota family of key suppliers.

As a result of the second world oil crisis in 1976 the Japanese began to realize that their 25-year pattern of continuous economic and manufacturing growth had been broken, and that in the future they would face peaks and valleys in manufacturing just like the Western nations do. The nation's manufacturing leaders looked for ways to increase the flexibility of their manufacturing processes, and came upon Toyota's system.

Since 1976, Just In Time has been spreading through more and more of Japan's manufacturing businesses. But JIT is still not dominant in Japanese manufacturing. Many Japanese companies are making the same mistakes implementing JIT as are Western companies, adding weight to the argument that JIT is not "Japanese" as such, but rather, universal principles of good manufacturing that have been well packaged by some Japanese manufacturers.

Around 1980 a few people in the United States got together and studied what the leading edge Japanese companies (especially Toyota) were doing to make them so successful. Our initial study identified 14 points. Seven of them had to do with what was termed "respect for people." The other seven had to do with the "elimination of waste," which is more technically oriented.

When thinking and talking about these 14 points, we lumped them together as the "Japanese Approach to Productivity."

We then studied the 14 points in more detail to determine which would be appropriate in the Western context and could be introduced into Western manufacturing. This analysis ended up focusing on 7 of the 14 points as being the most appropriate for the West. These seven points make up the essential elements now referred to as "Just In Time." We also came to the startling realization that, in one form or another, most of these supposedly Japanese concepts came from the United States.

This necessitated a change in focus from the "Japanese Approach to Productivity" to "Just-In-Time Production." However, the emphasis was still on Japan, because at that time Japan was providing the only examples of JIT working successfully.

The constant references to Japanese quality, Japanese productivity, and now Japanese manufacturing excellence in the form of Just In Time began to take their toll in some quarters, demonstrating the truth of Mark Twain's observation that "Few things are harder to put up with than the annoyance of a good example."

This has become less and less a problem as the West has produced an increasing number of its own good examples of JIT success stories.

With the automotive industry as a catalyst—through the Automotive Industry Action Group (AIAG)—Just In Time began to be used in North America. Outside the automotive industry, Omark Industries, Black and Decker, and Hewlett Packard are among the best known of JIT's early North American implementers.

The philosophy began to filter into Canada and Europe, mostly through divisions of U.S.-based corporations, around 1982 or 1983, and around 1985 it began to show up in South and Central America, again through divisions of U.S. corporations.

Now it is no longer necessary to dwell on Japanese companies as the only examples. In fact, it is time to eliminate references to Japan from discussions of JIT whenever possible. Just In Time is a manufacturing philosophy that has truly arrived in the West.

THE SEVEN ELEMENTS OF JUST IN TIME

Let's talk a little bit more about the seven elements of the Japanese approach to productivity that we found that can be used in the West. There are six different internally focused elements and one externally focused element. (See Fig. 1.1.)

The first internally focused element is the Just-In-Time philosophy itself. The second is quality at the source. There are three manufacturing engineering elements: uniform plant load, overlapping operations (machine cells or group technology), and minimum setup time. The sixth internally focused element is a type of control system called, variously, a pull system, Kanban, or linking operations.

The externally focused element is Just-In-Time purchasing.

CREATING A WESTERN JIT

Up to this point in our U.S. development, we had progressed from 14 elements of Japanese productivity to 7 elements focused on JIT. But how did we get from there to our current level of understanding—that JIT is composed of three basic components?

First, we determined that the JIT philosophy—the elimination of waste—is really the lynchpin of the entire JIT phenomenon, so that was pulled out of the seven elements and put on top as the umbrella under which everything else fit. The remaining six elements are really techniques and approaches to accomplishing the elimination of waste.

Second, we realized that the six elements are not all of equal importance.

Quality is a major theme. However, since Western manufacturers had already started to focus on questions of quality and had already been indoctrinated into many of the techniques of quality, we did not list every technique of quality as a separate element of JIT. Quality, which has been a separate topic for both the Japanese and Western manufacturers for a number of years, is the second basic component to successful JIT. However, while quality does not absolutely need JIT, JIT certainly needs quality.

The other five elements—uniform plant load, overlapping operations, reduced setup time, purchasing, and a pull system—all are techniques. These were lumped together in a group. But the group had no theme.

Looking at our equation at this point we had a skewed picture—one theme without elements and five elements without a theme.

In order to help organize our arrangement somewhat, we determined that the five techniques could be categorized together as techniques of flow; that is, the way the manufacturing process proceeds from one operation to the next.

Now we had our seven elements of JIT more logically organized. Yet something seemed missing. That something was a part of JIT that we could not separate out as an element, because it was all-pervasive—it needed to be infused in every element of JIT to make JIT work. That missing ingredient was human resources, employee involvement. The reason we were so slow to realize this was missing was that employee involvement is a given in the Japanese culture, something Japanese manufacturing managers didn't even have to think about when they were working with JIT. But in the West, the culture of employee involvement, of teamwork, must be developed in a company in order for JIT to work.

The first two components of JIT—flow and quality—will be dealt with in the first part of the book. Each element that has been incorporated into the flow component will be dealt with in its own chapter. Although quality is as big a subject as flow, it will be dealt with in only one chapter because there are already so many books about quality.

Employee involvement will be dealt with mainly in the second part of the book, the four chapters devoted to implementation.

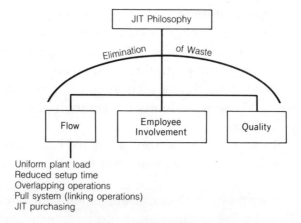

Figure 1.1.   The JIT Philosophy

BEST OF THE EAST, BEST OF THE WEST

With all this rethinking of the Japanese methods of production and the creation of what is hoped will be a truly Westernized JIT, it becomes clear that Western manufacturers should not slavishly be copying Japan—but using the best of the East and the best of the West to create a new manufacturing philosophy that will make Western manufacturers not only competitive, but the best in the world.

The Japanese, especially JIT companies, excel at perfect execution of a plan. Westerners excel at quick reactions, thinking on their feet, and replanning. Part of the reason we Westerners excel at replanning, however, is because we are often bad at carrying out the original plan.

If Western manufacturing can get part way as good as the Japanese at carrying out plans and at fine tuning this balance and flow, while at the same time maintaining the ability to think on their feet, they will be able to use their advantage more effectively. That is really the goal of JIT in the Western context—to take the best from the Japanese without giving up any of the good things about Western manufacturing.

WHAT IS JUST IN TIME?

Just-In-Time Production In Its Simplest Terms

The JIT philosophy, when carried out properly, reduces or eliminates major amounts of waste from the purchasing, manufacturing, distribution, and manufacturing support (office) activities of
any manufacturing business. This is done using the three basic
components of flow, quality, and employee involvement. First, it
is necessary to have a working definition of waste. Toyota, the
originator of the JIT concept, defines waste as "anything other
than the minimum amount of equipment, materials, parts, and
working time absolutely essential to production."

I spent a long time thinking about how we could "Westernize"
the concept of eliminating waste in order to make it more under-
standable within the Western cultural context. The solution I
came upon is the American idea of adding value, which was introduced to manufacturing through value analysis and value engineering. Manufacturers should be asking, What is it that adds
value to the product?

The reason for talking about adding value is that it helps take
away the subjectivity of the part of the Toyota definition that
talks about "absolutely essential." Adding value gives us a hard
and fast test to use as a benchmark, rather than depending on the
term "absolutely essential to production." After all, it can be ar-
gued as to what is essential. If the Japanese can all agree on what
is essential, that is wonderful—although I believe the fact that so
many Japanese companies are having trouble implementing JIT
means they cannot agree on what is essential.

Adding Value: The American Definition

The American definition of waste, which I developed by modifying the Toyota definition to deal with value added, is: "Anything other than the absolute minimum resources of material,
machines, and manpower required to add value to the product."

Absolute Minimum Resources

Most Western manufacturers think they already work with minimum resources; they lay people off during slow times and have major justification processes for approving new equipment. This may be the American concept of minimum resources. But it is not truly minimum resources as intended in this definition. It is only through use of absolute minimum resources that manufacturing can become truly efficient.

What do I mean by absolute minimum resources? Some examples of absolute minimum resources are:

One supplier, if that supplier has enough capacity

No people, equipment, or space dedicated to rework

No safety stock

No excess lead times

No people doing jobs that don't add value

The Western concept of efficient manufacturing starts with speed. The idea is that the faster something can be produced, the cheaper it must be. Therefore, we Westerners go for horsepower and speed, not absolute minimum resources.

Westerners also insist on safety—contingency—to be able to ship and keep people working even when things go wrong. Westerners like to feel that if anything goes wrong—and things will go wrong—people and equipment can be kept busy doing something while the problem is worked out. Because of this, Western manufacturing needs extra inventory, capacity, and manpower. This takes them about as far away from minimum resources as they could possibly get.

Adding Value

The second, and maybe even more important, part of the definition is adding value. *Only an activity that physically changes the product adds value.*

In the machining business, for example, every new cut adds value. Plating and heat treating add value. Assembly adds value. In other businesses mixing, melting, molding, soldering, weaving, and sterilizing add value. In a consumer business, packaging adds value because it increases the value in the eyes of the customer.

But what about all the other things that traditionally happen in the manufacturing process? Counting a product does not add value to it. Moving something does not add value. In fact, moving is an opportunity to lose value—through damage. Storing something does not add value. Transferring something from a large container to a small container does not add value.

Remembering the rule about physically changing a product, even inspection does not add value. Inspection will tell whether a value-adding step has been done properly, but the action itself does not add value. In a similar way, scheduling something does not directly add value to it.

All of these things add cost, but not value. They are wastes. Anything that is identified as a waste, because it does not directly add value to the product, should be put on a list and nailed to the wall. Those are the targets for elimination. That does not mean JIT has yet developed ways to eliminate all of those wastes. But it is amazing how many of these activities companies are learning how to reduce or eliminate now that they have been defined as wastes.

VALUE-ADDED ANALYSIS

Conducting a value-added analysis is an important part of finding out what Just-In-Time manufacturing can do for a company. For many people, it is truly a waking-up exercise. The value-added analysis shows them, perhaps for the first time, how truly inefficient the traditional manufacturing process is.

The proper way to do a value-added analysis is to take a pad and pencil and go out onto the shop floor. Do not get a routing sheet to see how the process is supposed to go. Instead, find a single product and follow it through the manufacturing process, tracking every activity performed on the product.

Exhibit 1-1 is an actual operation sheet for a machined part, showing eight operations. After the eighth operation, putting the part in stock as a blank, it comes out of stock, goes through seven more operations to be made into any one of a half dozen potential parts, is put back in stock and then removed from stock to be put into one of a number of different assemblies. In total, 19 operations are performed on the part before it is packed and shipped. We will focus on the first eight, however, until it goes into stock the first time as a blank.

Exhibit 1-2 is a value-added analysis that shows not just the eight operations, but 75 activities. Only three of these activities (in fact, only three of the eight operations) add value, using the JIT definition. The others are all wastes.

EXHIBIT 1-1
Operation Sheet
Machined Part (blank)

Operation No.	Description
1	Form, drill, tap, and cutoff
2	Inspect
3	Drill and tap upper
4	Degrease
5	Drill and tap lower
6	Degrease
7	Inspect
8	To stock

EXHIBIT 1-2
Value-Added Activity Analysis
Machined Part (blank)

Activity No.	Operation No.	Description	Adds Value
1	1	Form, drill, tap, cutoff into pan	X
2		Wait (until pan full)	
3		Place pan onto skid	
4		Wait (until end of lot or end of shift)	
5		Move to cleaning area incoming	
6		Wait	
7		Transfer into wash basket	
8		Wash	
9		Transfer into tote pan	
10		Place on skid	
11		Wait (for rest of lot)	
12		Move to weigh-count area	
13		Wait (until end of shift)	
14		Load onto scale	
15		Weigh-count	
16		Return to skid	
17		Document	
18		Wait (for rest of lot)	
19		Move to inspection area	
20		Wait	
21	2	Inspect	

EXHIBIT 1-2 (continued)

Activity No.	Operation No.	Description	Adds Value
22		Document	
23		Wait	
24		Move to dept. 16 incoming	
25		Wait	
26		Move to G&D machine	
27		Load G&D machine	
28	3	Drill and tap upper	X
---		...	
42	4	Degrease	
---		...	
50	5	Drill and tap lower	X
---		...	
64	6	Degrease	
---		...	
70	7	Inspect	
---		...	
75	8	To stock	

Although this example deals with a metalworking process, the same is true of all industries. Exhibit 1-3 shows examples from our client list.

Not only will the techniques of JIT manufacturing help eliminate some of the non-value-added steps in any of these industries, but these techniques will work in any environment—repetitive manufacturing, process industries, or job shops. In addition to working in manufacturing support areas (offices) of manufacturing companies, JIT techniques can be applied to nonmanufacturing companies.

EXHIBIT 1-3
Value-Added Activity List
Seven Industries

Industry	Steps	Value-Added Steps	% Steps Value Added
Glass (tableware)	72	6	8
Food (ingredient proc.)	37	4	11
Textile (yarn mfg. and weaving)	105	11	10
Metal (wheel cylinder)	187	13	7
Electronics (cable assembly)	239	19	8
Consumer products (disposable razor)	105	10	10
Mfg. support (order entry)	98	15	15

If the fact that only 8 to 11 percent of the steps in any manufacturing operation add value seems bad, the ratio of time during the manufacturing process that is actually used to add value versus time that is spent in waste activities is even worse.

JIT does not only work to eliminate non-value-adding steps so that a higher percentage of manufacturing steps add value, but JIT helps insure that a far larger portion of manufacturing time is spent on tasks that actually add value. Most companies find that value-adding manufacturing steps actually take up less than one half of one percent of all the time an item spends in the manufacturing process.

There is a simple test any company can do to indicate how little value-added time is spent on any product it makes.

For example, we performed such a test for a company that

manufactures shafts for one of our clients, Xerox. The cost of each shaft is made up of $5 for purchased materials and $5 of cost the company adds in the manufacturing process. Let's assume that all the added cost is value-added—although in reality it may not be.

The lead time for this product is two weeks—not at all unreasonable. That means the company takes $5 of materials and, over two weeks, adds $5 of value. The company works two shifts. That means the item is in-house for 160 hours—40 hours per week times two shifts per week (80 hours) times two weeks (160 hours). The hourly wage of manufacturing workers at this company averages about $8 per hour. That means the value added ($5) represents less than the equivalent of 40 minutes of paid labor. JIT asks the question: Why does it require running the manufacturing facility for 160 hours in order to add the equivalent of 40 minutes of labor? Forty minutes is less than one half of one percent of the total time the item is in the company's manufacturing process.

It is no wonder that companies implementing JIT whose goal is to eliminate non-value-adding steps have lead time reductions of 80 to 90 percent. In theory, they should be able to reduce throughput time by 99.5 percent.

The concept of adding value is so integral that I will use it many times in this book. At the end of many of the technical chapters in the first part of the book, I will go through a value-added analysis of a real-life case—taking out the company name—showing how a Rath and Strong client has eliminated waste steps by successfully implementing one of the JIT techniques.

JIT BENEFITS

I've spoken about the benefits of JIT in the abstract. Exhibit 1-4 shows some of the more tangible results of JIT and the elimination of waste in the manufacturing process. The figures represent ranges of improvement gained by our clients in a number of different industries. Some of these improvements convert directly to dollars, while others are more obviously improvements in service to customers.

EXHIBIT 1-4
JIT Opportunities

	Range of Improvement (%)
Lead-time reduction	83–92
Productivity increase	
Direct labor	5–50
Indirect/salary	21–60
Cost of quality reduction	26–63
Purchased material price reduction	6–45
Inventory reduction	
Purchased material	35–73
Work in process	70–89
Finished goods	0–90
Setup reduction	75–94
Space reduction	39–80

WASTE NOT, WANT NOT: THE IMPORTANCE OF FLOW AND QUALITY

One of the central tenets of Just In Time—flow—says, in effect, that Henry Ford was right. Not his Model T, but rather the concept of the assembly line. Henry Ford and his people thought up and developed the assembly line around the turn of the twentieth century. The actual name "assembly line" was given to the idea later, and was derived from the fact that the parts and components were put together in sequence—or "assembled" to the frame—as the frame moved along a line in which there was balance, synchronization, and uninterrupted flow.

The Henry Ford concept of balance, synchronization, and flow can be applied to an entire assembly line, a machine cell, or even an administrative flow of work in an office.

Henry Ford's creation of an assembly line is very close to the concept of Just In Time as developed by Toyota. In fact, an entire chapter in the Toyota employee handbook is dedicated to Ford and the assembly line concept he created at Ford Motor Company. (See Fig. 2.1.)

Way back in the 1960s, Toyota tried to encapsulate and embrace this Henry Ford concept in a definition. Again, I have reworked the original Toyota definition so that it fits better with both Western grammar and Western conditions. My modification of the Toyota definition of Just-In-Time production (or an assembly line) is: "the smallest possible quantity at the latest possible time and the elimination of inventory."

The assembly line uses the smallest possible quantity. Even if the order quantity is a million units, and the assembly line is in the process of making these million units, it is moving these units one at a time from operation to operation and each operation has only one unit.

The assembly line works at the latest possible time. Operation two is completed and ready for operation three exactly when operation three needs it. If operation three stops needing that unit, operation two stops producing it.

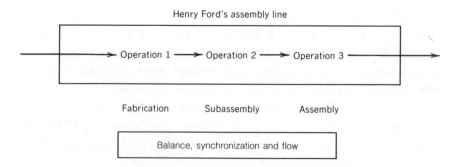

Figure 2.1.   Henry Ford's Assembly Line

Inventories must be eliminated because they are the greatest hindrance to flow.

It is necessary to keep in mind that, once again, what is being presented here is a picture of perfection. No company has reached this level of perfection—not even Toyota—throughout their manufacturing process. However, any company can achieve perfection in some parts of its manufacturing process by implementing the philosophy, concepts, and techniques of Just In Time.

Although talking about perfection may seem unrealistic, it is necessary to understand what perfection is so that it is possible to see in what direction a company must move. Then it is possible to take step by practical step in that direction, constantly working toward perfection.

An assembly line—or any sequence of events or operations—that has balance, synchronization, and flow has little if any waste activity. Products are not counted between operations. Neither are they put into containers. Containers are not moved to warehouses and stored, because they do not exist as such. Products do not have to be taken out of containers and put back on the assembly line for the next operation because they were never in containers in the first place. None of the work usually associated with a batch-type environment—except for the actual operations—happens on an assembly line.

One of the more unique eliminations of waste associated with an assembly line environment is derived from the reduced need for scheduling. In a batch-type environment, each individual operation has to be scheduled. However, an assembly line is scheduled as a whole, usually through master scheduling to customer requirements. The individual operations within the assembly line schedule themselves, or more precisely, control themselves when the line is balanced and synchronized.

A considerable portion of this book is devoted to the discussion and explanation of this concept and the techniques embodied in it.

SPEED

Consider for a minute the impact of speed on an assembly line. Consider what would happen if it became possible to speed up by some 40 percent one of the operations somewhere in the middle of an assembly line. What would be the reason for doing that? If that was all there was to it, what would be gained? The operator at that particular operation would simply have 40 percent more time on his hands to do what? Sit and do nothing! And in total, no more comes off the line.

Now think about speeding up the first operation. Assuming it is possible to keep the first operation supplied with enough material to keep it busy, it will be producing 40 percent too fast for the rest of the line, and an out-of-balance situation will quickly develop.

The additional output of that operation would have to be offloaded, stored, handled, accounted for, scheduled back into the line, as well as whatever other administrative work would be required. In the end, that operation would need to be pulled off the line and given space to itself that wasn't needed before, as well as containers, material handlers, and administrators that weren't needed before.

BALANCE AND SYNCHRONIZATION

It is easy to see what has happened. By speeding up one of the operations in the line to make that operation more efficient, the real cost of the product through the assembly line as a whole would be increased, but no additional product would come out of the end of the line.

Adding to the speed of an individual operation within an assembly line would severely disrupt the balance, synchronization, and flow of that line. It is easy to understand that balance, synchronization, and flow are good and that they should not be disrupted, because in the long run such an environment is worth more to us in the form of consistently improved operations as the process is refined and fine tuned. It is not difficult to see and understand that if something is already in balance it is not good to disrupt that balance.

Just In Time says that the assembly line is probably the most effective (as opposed to efficient—which implies speed) way to produce products. It also says that the principles governing assembly line processes should be applied to the entire manufacturing and operations process as well: the assembly department, subassembly, the fabrication process, and even the purchasing and distribution processes by involving first, a company's suppliers and second, a company's major customers directly in its process.

One way to describe Just In Time is as a collection of old ideas and new techniques to be used in combination in order to establish balance, synchronization, and flow in those areas of the manufacturing process where Western companies have not yet done so.

If the company is a job shop, it can flow in some parts much more like a repetitive manufacturer. If the company is a repetitive manufacturer, parts of the process can flow like a process industry. For those companies that are already process industries, they can flow more completely and more flexibly using Just In Time.

A booklet from 1924 about the Ford Motor Company describes the manufacturing process. The booklet explains how the iron ore boat docked on Monday morning at the River Rouge plant in Detroit, how that iron ore was smelted into iron, resmelted with scrap into steel, and poured into molds for engine blocks. Engine blocks were then cooled, machined, assembled into an engine, tested, transported to the automobile assembly plant, assembled into an automobile, and delivered. In 1924 the manufacturing time from raw ore to a finished and delivered car was 48 hours. Where did U.S. manufacturing go wrong?

One of the things that Just In Time is doing is getting manufacturing back to that kind of flow and balance and synchronization despite the fact that the 1980s are not like the 1920s. Manufacturers no longer have a marketplace that allows them to say, "You can have any color you want so long as it is black." The 1980s demand a constant flow of new products and a tremendous number of options, all with little or no inventory or lead time.

In the next four chapters, I will tie together the various techniques of flow—uniform plant load, reduction of setup time, overlapping operations in machine cells, and linking operations in a pull system. These constitute the internal technical elements of Just In Time.

QUALITY

Another concept is not only equal in importance to balance, synchronization, and flow, but is considered to be second in importance only to the actual philosophy of Just In Time. It is the concept of quality at the source, of doing it right the first time throughout all areas of the organization.

Just In Time demands quality. Strong words indeed. However, without quality in the form of prevention before the fact, it is difficult to achieve balance, synchronization, and flow to any significant degree. There can be no producing at the latest possible time, and therefore no chance of reaching the vision of the future afforded by Just In Time.

INVENTORY

Part of the definition of Just-In-Time production concerns itself with the elimination of inventory. This part of the definition has led as much as anything else to the misconception that Just In Time is an inventory reduction program.

The real question behind the elimination of inventories is "Why?"

It is necessary for a company to understand why it is important to eliminate inventory before worrying about how to do it.

A lot of people think the rationale behind eliminating inventory is that inventory costs money. It is true that inventory costs money to carry, and reducing these costs is certainly beneficial to the company. There are much data available showing that inventory carrying costs generally equal 25 to 30 percent of the inventory value.

However, while an important goal of Just In Time is the reduction of real cost, it is not the reason Just In Time wants companies to reduce or eliminate inventory.

That reason is that inventory is *inherently evil*. It is bad for the manufacturing process.

Why is this? Why is inventory evil?

Because inventory hides problems. Traditional manufacturers have long thought of inventory as protecting them and their customers against problems. However, the Just-In-Time philosophy shows companies that exactly the opposite is true.

Inventory actually protects problems from people solving them. By providing operational buffers and/or safety stocks throughout the process—and in finished goods—manufacturers prevent problems from being solved. Such inventory covers problems up and provides manufacturers with ways simply to live better with the problems so they don't need to solve problems. It has become an institutionalized way of life for traditional manufacturers to be prepared through the use of inventory rather than by solving the problems that cause them to need inventory.

ROCKS AND WATER

The Japanese and Western practitioners of Just In Time talk about "rocks and water." Rocks are symbolic of all problems. Water is symbolic of the inventory that traditionalists use to protect and buffer themselves from these problems—the inventory used to cover up problems.

As an example, think of a machine that has a history of breaking down two or three times a day for 10 to 15 minutes at a time, and it has been doing this since anyone can remember. Long ago it became a real hindrance to operations. Equally long ago a policy was established to buffer that machine, and others like it, with inventory so these hindrances would not hurt or interrupt the rest of the process.

Today, years later, that machine is still breaking down three or four times a day for 10 to 15 minutes each time. Now, however, no one is directly aware of it except the operator trying to run the machine and the person from maintenance who is called upon time after time to fix it. The inventory buffer has become an institutionalized way of life, and protects or hides the problem from everyone except the operator and the repair person.

No one else is aware of the problem because it has no visible impact on the rest of the process. In such an environment that problem will never be solved. The process will stay at its current level of cost and efficiency, not getting the best utilization from the equipment or the people, and it will take constant attention to repair it and inventory to buffer it to protect the rest of the process from delays and stops.

Now multiply this by the number of operations throughout the plant and it is possible to get an idea of how much inventory is involved in buffering operations, how much time this inventory sits idle waiting to be worked on, and therefore what opportunities would be available if the problems were solved and the reasons for the inventory eliminated.

Given this long history of an artificially high inventory necessary to buffer and protect against problems, a company must think carefully about how to start restructuring its operations in order to reduce these inventories.

A number of people who visit Japan and observe the operations in their factories return and say that dropping the water level—in other words arbitrarily reducing inventory—is the way to expose problems so that these problems can be solved.

These people miss a very important point: The Japanese are substantially ahead of the rest of the world in problem solving. Most Westerners tend to forget that the Japanese have been solving problems—quality problems and other problems—for more than 25 years. The Japanese can afford to crank down the inventory to see what happens because by comparison their problems are relatively small ones and therefore following this path does not jeopardize either their operations or their customer relationships.

If traditionally managed Western companies suddenly dropped their inventory levels to expose problems, most would find the problems overwhelming to the point of causing major shutdowns.

For years, as Western manufacturers have found problems they have increased inventories. What needs to be done is exactly the opposite; when problems are found they must be solved once and for all so inventories can be reduced. (See Fig. 2.2.)

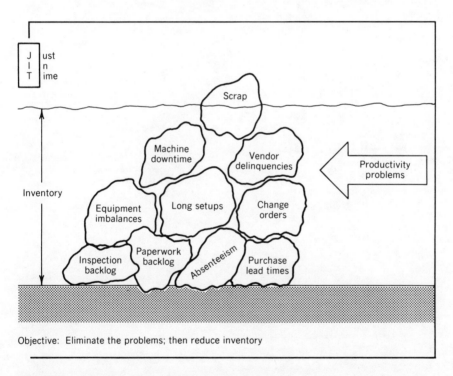

Figure 2.2.   Just-In-Time Objective: Eliminate The Problems; then Reduce Inventory

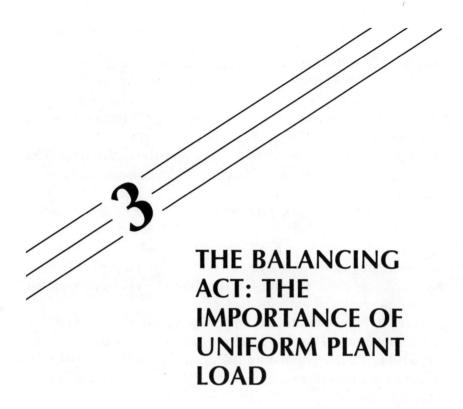

THE BALANCING ACT: THE IMPORTANCE OF UNIFORM PLANT LOAD

Of the three basic components for eliminating waste—activities that do not add value—the one unique to Just In Time (JIT) is the concept of balance, synchronization, and flow. The JIT philosophy states that balance is required for flow and that balance, therefore, is of prime importance, even more important than speed. One of the first logical questions then becomes: What should be balanced to what? This question is answered by the concept of uniform plant load.

Uniform plant load introduces two ideas. One is "cycle time," which deals with the rate of production. The other is "level loading," which deals with the frequency of production.

In JIT, cycle time does not mean the same thing that an industrial engineer might use it to mean—the time it takes a piece of equipment to do its thing. Cycle time under JIT is a measure of the rate of requirement—often measured by the rate of sales. The principle of cycle time states that the production rate must equal the requirement rate.

When I say this, most production people say, "What else is new? We do that. Occasionally we build ahead, we produce more than we know we need, more than we know we can sell. We are getting ready for a shutdown or a seasonal push. We have a capacity problem. But most of the time we set our production rate at our requirement rate."

In reality, however, these companies are not producing to the requirement rate. They are producing at the machine rate (as fast as possible). These companies then make a one-time adjustment to their requirement rate by turning the machine off when they have enough.

Cycle time says that production should not be equal to the ability to produce. Rather, production should be keyed to what is needed.

Picture being able to put a rheostat on every piece of equipment—every assembly line, every bench operation, every machine. These rheostats can be dialed up or dialed down. When the requirement rate is established by customer demand or master schedule, it is almost as if someone in the company can physically go from rheostat to rheostat and adjust each particular line or operation so that it now runs at the correct number of pieces per hour—dial this one up, this one down, this one down, this one up.

Admittedly, this is an exercise in imagination, a picture of perfection. However, it is possible to come very close to this imagined perfection, and it is not difficult to do if taken one step at a time.

START WITH THE LAST OPERATION

Cycle time should be implemented with the last operation first. The requirement rate at the last operation will be, in most cases, the customer requirement. Once the theoretical rheostat is set, the production rate of the last operation becomes the requirement rate of the feeding operations. Continuing to work backward in the process, each feeding operation can be examined and the rheostats set for those operations. The object is to keep the flow smooth, producing only at the rate required by the next step in the process.

When companies analyze their rates of demand and production at different steps in their manufacturing process, they most often find that they are doing exactly the opposite.

THE YO-YO ANALYSIS

The way to measure requirements at different levels of the process—demand variability—is through what is called the "yo-yo analysis."

Those requirements coming in from the customer, whoever the customer is, have variations from one period to another. We measure the requirements at the master scheduling level and find that the variation has amplified in the assembly/subassembly process. At the component manufacturing level it is amplified some more. At the supplier level it is even more amplified. All starting with the customer requirement.

Often, the customer uses a product daily but it is assembled and shipped weekly, the necessary components are made monthly, and the raw materials are purchased quarterly.

The requirement is amplified through a company's processes by things the company considers economical—running each operation as fast as possible, producing in economical (large) lots, and building in safety stocks and safety lead times. Thus a smooth requirement at the last operation turns into a lumpy and often unpredictable requirement at the first operation.

What Just In Time is trying to do is to take a requirement for a specific period of time—it might be a month, a week, or two weeks, but most often we talk about a month—make the best possible analysis of that requirement, divide it by the number of working days in the period, and determine what the average requirement is for each day. Ideally, every day in a period will then be the same.

Then by introducing the concept of cycle time at the assembly level, Just In Time assures that the requirement at the subassembly level is also as smooth as possible throughout the period. If this can be done at the subassembly level, the pull—or requirement—at the component level will be exactly the same. Carrying this through the entire process, the requirement will be as level at the supplier level as it can possibly be. Now a reasonable requirement can stay reasonable throughout the levels of the distribution, manufacturing, and purchasing processes.

SETTING THE RATE

This rate can be expressed either traditionally, as units per hour, or as seconds per unit if it is a low-volume item. The example in Figure 3.1 shows both: 200 units per hour and one unit every 18 seconds.

The idea is to get back to Henry Ford's assembly line, imagining, however, that the last operation is the cash register. If the cash register is going at the rate of 200 sales per hour—or one sale every 18 seconds—there is no value added to the process or the organization in speeding up the assembly line to produce any faster than that. In fact, doing so will only add waste into the process and cost into the product.

Let us go through an example applying the concept of cycle time to the last operation, typically an assembly line, for a one-month production period (Figure 3.1).

Figure 3.1 shows the February requirements, 32,000 units spread over four different products. The bottom of Figure 3.1 shows the calculated cycle time requirement of 200 units per hour—one unit every 18 seconds—for the month.

This particular example is of an assembly line that was originally engineered to have the capability of producing 400 units per hour—one unit every nine seconds. It normally runs with a crew of 10 people. (Figure 3.1, line 1).

Ideally, under Just In Time, the company would reengineer that line so that it only produces 200 units per hour—one every 18 seconds—because that is what the demand is (Figure 3.2, line 2).

Since the output of this line is being cut in half to meet February's demand, the crew size should also be reduced by an equal percentage (to five operators) so labor cost remains constant.

As difficult as this sounds, it is only the beginning, because the same calculations must be made again every month. Just In Time wants a company to engineer the line so that it is sufficiently flexible to produce each month exactly what is required, using more or less labor so that the labor cost per unit remains constant even though the demand varies.

The way to calculate crew size is to use the current standard—in this case one unit every nine seconds, or 400 units per hour with 10 people. The direct labor content of each unit is 90

Figure 3.1:
Assembly Line Cycle Time

Model	February Requirement
A	16,000
B	10,000
C	4,000
D	2,000
Total	32,000

÷ 20 days = 1600/day
÷ 8 hours = 200/hour,
or 1 every 18 seconds

Figure 3.2:

Cycle Time/Crew Size Matrix—Three Months

	Requirement Per Mo.	Requirement Per Hr.	Cycle Time	Crew Size	Labor Content
Original standard	64,000	400	9.0	10	90
February	32,000	200	18.0	5	90
March	38,400	240	15.0	6	90
April	25,600	160	22.5	4	90

seconds (400 units per hour is one unit every nine seconds times 10 people working equals 90 seconds of direct labor per unit.) For 200 units per hour—18 seconds per unit—in order to produce each unit with 90 seconds of direct labor, five people must be used. The labor content must remain stable.

If for the following month 240 units per hour are required—no more, no less—six people will be needed to meet this requirement and maintain the direct-labor content per unit of 90 seconds.

This is considerably easier to do in theory than in practice. It is not at all easy to do this with most of today's manufacturing lines. A special kind of physical layout is required to have this flexibility and be able to accommodate varying crew sizes based on demand in order to keep labor cost per unit constant. We will discuss the principles of such a layout in Chapter 5.

THREE QUESTIONS

Three major questions jump into people's minds when they think about reengineering lines in order to vary output rates and crew sizes.

1. What happens to people?
2. Isn't there one most efficient balance to any given line?
3. What happens to the absorption of fixed costs if equipment is run at a slower speed?

I like to deal with these questions in reverse order.

What happens to the absorption of fixed costs if equipment is run at slower speed? The answer to this is simple: Absolutely nothing changes! Fixed costs are always recovered by what is produced and sold. Regardless of whether JIT is being used, the amount produced and sold in February will be 32,000 units.

However, if the cost accounting system measures fixed cost absorption by the hour or by the unit, slower run speeds will indeed make it *look* like there is a problem; fixed costs will appear to be underabsorbed, and performance reports will show negative variances. However, if accounting will measure fixed cost absorption on a period basis—if period costs are measured by the period rather than by the hour or the unit—there will be no problem. Fixed costs will be properly absorbed.

Isn't there one best balance? The answer, of course, is no. Under Just In Time there is not one best balance. Our consulting experience has shown that given the right physical layout, there are several equally effective balances possible for any given production line.

However, even if there were one most efficent balance in terms of use of labor, it certainly would not be the original standard in the example—10 people operating at 400 units per hour. This is because currently U.S. manufacturers do not man lines based on the most effective use of labor. Rather, lines are manned to get maximum hourly output. In short, the question should not be how many people have to be put on a line to make it go as fast as possible, but rather, how fast does the line have to run, and how many people are necessary, to make the number of units needed by the customer for this production month.

What happens to people? This is really a two-part question.

The first part is the initial redesign question: What happens to the five people who have always been used on the line but suddenly are not going to be there in February?

The second part is the month-to-month questions: Where do the people go and where do they come from month to month as production requirements vary? And, does cycle time ask that people be hired and fired more frequently than the current norm?

The Redesign Question: What Happens to the Five People?

Remember, the line has been engineered to produce twice as fast as the product is being consumed. Therefore the line can run only half of the available time now and the people on that line are only needed half the time.

So the real question is: What currently happens to the 10 people during the 50 percent of the time they are not on the line?

Do they run the line in the morning and get reassigned in the afternoon? Do they run the line every second day and get reassigned the other days? Perhaps they run the line for three months and pile up three months worth of inventory, then they get laid off for the next three months. No matter how it is done, the workers are only on the line half the time.

Pacing the line to the demand by implementing the Just-In-Time concept of cycle time converts the 10 half-time jobs into five full-time jobs. Whatever those 10 people did with the other half of their time can now be done by the five people who are not needed on the line in February.

The Second Part: Month-By-Month Needs

The answer to the second part of the question is: No, cycle time does not ask that people be hired and fired more frequently. However, it does ask that there be frequent assignment and reassignment—in this case monthly—on and off certain tasks as required so that productivity will match demand, inventories will be nonexistent, and labor costs will be constant.

What I am talking about here is not a change in the work force for the entire facility, only for the line. It is meant to cope with changes in mix—not business levels. JIT wants to have a stable total work force. One of the best ways to ensure this is flexibility, the ability to assign and reassign—to shift workers to where the production is needed.

Flexibility has not been, and is not now, one of the hallmarks of the U.S. work force. Over the past half century, management–worker relationships and the traditional management style have produced a work force that is fairly rigid, inflexible, and often "protected" from having to do a number of varying jobs by negotiated work rules that are part of union contracts, or by longstanding industry traditions and precedents. Traditional manufacturers have done little to stress flexibility, opting instead to maintain the status quo and, they hope, to achieve a level of labor peace by doing so.

The concept of flexibility in the work force, where people can do varied jobs that may in fact cross basic skill areas, is really two separate issues. The first issue is that of developing an attitude among the people in the work force such that they are willing to be trained and become flexible. Just In Time seeks to foster an attitude in the work force that says it is okay for a person to be asked to work on one job one month and another job another month.

This, of course, will require that a different set of management–work force relationships be developed. It also means that different work rules will have to be put in place with regard to such issues as job descriptions, job rates, bumping rules, transfers, and the like. The ideal that companies should be working toward is one job description, one class, and one pay rate for all work; sort of an egalitarian work force, yet one that encourages and rewards creativity and individual participation.

The second issue associated with flexibility of the work force is the actual ability of individuals to perform many tasks, and perform them well across varying skills areas. This includes being able to physically perform the jobs without causing quality problems, ruining tools, damaging machinery and equipment, or increasing the real cost of the product.

For example, assemblers of large capital equipment such as molding machines, stamping presses, or mining screens will need to become skilled in electricals, electronics, welding, mechanics, hydraulics, and metalwork in order to be assemblers. Today, manufacturing has people who are electrical assemblers, electronic assemblers, or mechanical assemblers, where the individual's work is for the most part limited to that specific skill area. Achieving this level of flexibility in the work force will take constant training and retraining over a substantial period of time.

Shifting the people around as the mix changes within the total demand—one line being dialed up and another line being dialed down—either from job to job or by changing content within the job, is the essence of work force flexibility.

LEVEL LOADING

Grant for the moment that the assembly line in our example, which was engineered to produce at twice the rate needed, has been reengineered so that it is now operating at cycle time—producing at the rate needed—200 units per hour, or one every 18 seconds. But what about each of the four product models the line produces? Is each product being produced as smoothly as possible and at the frequency it is required? Probably not.

Traditional manufacturing would note that model A represents 50 percent of what is needed from that line, so the line would be set up for production of model A for the first 50 percent of the month to produce a month's worth of model A. Then the line would be changed over to make a month's worth of model B, then a month's worth of model C, and so forth.

But if this were done, model A would not be produced as it is needed. The company is producing A's in 10 days that are being sold in 20 days, twice as fast as they are needed. B's are probably produced at six or seven times the speed at which they are needed.

This introduces the JIT concept of level loading (see Figs. 3.3 and 3.4), which focuses on the product itself. Cycle time gets the equipment running at the right speed—the need rate. Load leveling deals with producing the products at the right *frequency*. The principle of level loading states that products must be produced as frequently as the customer requires. In the extreme, if the item is sold every day it should be made every day.

In our example, this would mean that every day a day's worth of A's should be made, followed by a day's worth of B's, then a day's worth of C's and finally a day's worth of D's. The next day, the line would do it all over again. Clearly this is a major departure from traditional manufacturing concepts, but it can be done.

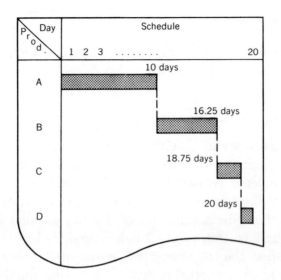

Figure 3.3. Level loading

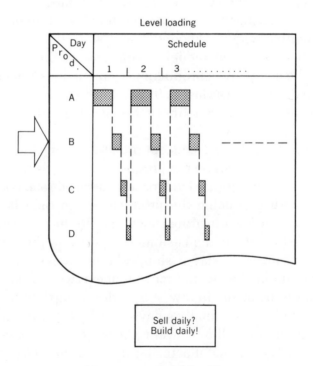

Figure 3.4. Level loading

46

The issue is how to get there. The goal is to produce smaller and smaller lots, so it is necessary to set up more frequently without incurring additional setup cost or equipment capacity loss.

The practical way to migrate from a month's worth every month to a day's worth every day is to learn to reduce the time of each individual setup, then reinvest the time saved into more frequent setups.

The line in our example is currently changing four times a month. Each setup takes x hours to accomplish (on average). If each setup time could be cut in half, then and only then should the line be willing to set up twice as often.

If changeovers are doubled, lot sizes can be halved. Instead of making a month's worth of each product model, the line can now make two week's worth. If setup time is cut in half again, then the line can set up four times as often and halve the lot sizes again. Note that all through this exercise equipment utilization stays the same. The total time for changeovers stays the same. That machine, or line, would still produce the same number of hours each month, but, on average, during the time it used to take to make a month's worth of one item it would now be making a week's worth of four different items. Nobody's ratios look worse, nobody sacrifices for the greater good, and there are no trade-offs of more setup time for lower inventory.

The work load for the operator stays the same. The work load for the setup people stays the same. However, in the amount of time it used to take to make one changeover, they are now able to make four.

Continuous improvement means that the big fix is not necessary. If it takes a year of small bites to get from making a month's worth every month to a day's worth every day, that is alright.

The notion of continous improvement is an integral part of the JIT philosophy. Americans, by nature, like the big-bang type of fix. We like to set an objective, work like crazy to meet that objective, and then move on to the next big objective—the next project in another area. What tends to happen is that the day the working like crazy stops, things begin to deteriorate back to where they were.

CONTINUOUS IMPROVEMENT

Getting from a month's worth every month to a week's worth every week requires a 75 percent reduction in setup time. Getting to daily production requires a 95 percent reduction. Such drastic reductions require full use of the JIT principle of continuous improvement.

The habit of continous improvement is like setting an objective of getting halfway to perfection. As soon as that is accomplished, set a new objective to get half of what is left. Mathematically, this is known is Xeno's paradox—if a person walks toward a wall, each step being half as large as the previous one, that person will never reach the wall. I may never get to the objective, but I keep working in that direction and am always thinking about how the process can be made better. In effect, I would like Western manufacturers to change their idea of problem solving from Pareto—getting 80 percent even if it means leaving 20 percent—to Xeno—continuously getting halfway to the goal.

Because of this principle of continuous improvement, the company gets into the mindset of improving everything all the time. To do this, it is necessary to get more people into the act. This is made possible by employee involvement and having many teams of employees at all levels of the organization working on solving problems. It provides many hands to share in the problem solving, and it lets companies tap all of their resources. It makes it possible to set an objective, meet that objective, and immediately set another objective.

BENEFITS OF LEVEL LOADING

The most important benefit of smaller and smaller lot sizes is that it lays the groundwork for level-by-level balance and flow by producing every product as smoothly and predictably as possible. Also, there are five other significant benefits a company can expect:

Learning curve improvements

Increased mix flexibility

Reduced inventory

Shorter lead times

Quality improvements

Learning Curve Improvements

As a company moves toward producing a day's worth every day, the nature of the learning curve changes. For example, an operator who makes a particular item for three days, then does not see it for another 17 days has three days to go up the learning curve, then 17 days to slide back down the learning curve. Producing that item every day practically eliminates any downside curve.

Also, a day's worth every day creates a completely different rhythm of production. Instead of falling into a pattern for a few days, then having life change, then getting into another pattern only to have things change again, every day is the same. Each day is more complicated in and of itself, but they are all alike. A day's worth of A's, changeover, a day's worth of B's, C's, and D's. The next day, exactly the same thing is done. There is a one-time learning curve to get from the old pattern to the new one, but once that is accomplished the day-to-day learning curve almost disappears.

Increased Mix Flexibility

If a customer calls in the middle of the production period, after all the A's and B's have been made for the month, and says he needs fewer A's and more B's, it is very difficult to accommodate that change. It is easy to ship fewer A's, but it is too late to produce fewer A's. And making more B's is a problem. If more B's are produced, it will not be at the expense of A's, but rather at the expense of C's and D's. The production of C's must be stopped and the pipeline filled with material for producing B's.

However, if a day's worth of each model is being produced each day, reaction to changes in mix can be almost immediate.

Reduced Inventory

The amount of work-in-process inventory is directly related to lot sizes. Every time lot sizes are cut in half, the average WIP inventory is also cut in half.

Finished goods inventory is also significantly reduced. In the average company most finished goods inventory is in the form of safety stock—stock that protects against changes in requirements between production runs. As the amount of time between production runs is reduced from a month to a day, the amount of possible change in requirements is drastically reduced.

Shorter Lead Times

As setup times are reduced and the shorter setup is translated into smaller lot sizes, lead times are also reduced. Lead times are not determined only by the amount or time it takes to manufacture something from the first operation to the last. Equally important is how often an item is produced. If a company is producing an item only once each month, it talks about lead times in terms of months. If the company is producing that item every week, it talks about lead times in terms of weeks.

Quality Improvements

Quality improvements result both from reducing setup time and from reducing lot sizes.

It is an established fact that the faster the setup, the better the setup—the better engineered it is and the more repeatable it is. There is much more consistency of product from lot to lot and within a lot. Production runs are smoother with far less need for adjustments during the run, and quality is more predictable.

Reducing lot sizes reduces the potential cost of rework or

scrap as the result of a defect that is not caught until after the lot is produced. Benefits accrue in a direct ratio—every time lot size is cut in half the potential cost of failure is also cut in half.

The two concepts of uniform plant load—running the equipment at the rate required and producing the product at the frequency required—are probably the two most radically different concepts of JIT. But they are key building blocks to establishing the level-by-level balance, synchronization, and flow throughout the manufacturing process that are critical in order to eliminate waste.

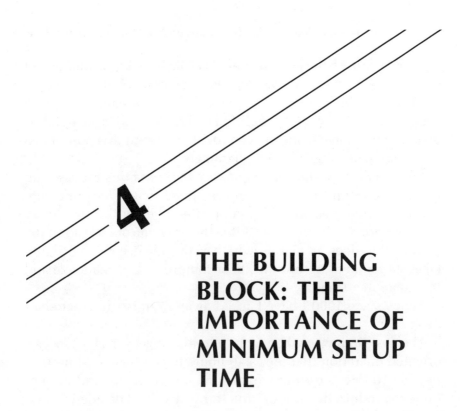

THE BUILDING BLOCK: THE IMPORTANCE OF MINIMUM SETUP TIME

Significant setup reduction is one of the basic requirements of any implementation of Just In Time. Reducing setups is needed to pave the way for every other element of JIT, from level loading to overlapping operations to pull systems and even to quality at the source.

In 1980 I went to Japan and studied the approach that several Japanese companies had been using, and are still using today, to reduce setups. I documented this approach and brought it back to North America to experiment with it. I had to find out first if the approach would work for all machines, and second, whether the approach could be successfully employed by a nontechnical person like me. The answer in both cases was yes.

As a result of these experiments, I have made a number of technical improvements, as well as some nontechnical changes, in order to Westernize the approach and formalize it into a specific process. Several years of hands-on successes on all kinds of equipment have made me confident enough at this point to issue a challenge and make a guarantee:

I will guarantee that any company that uses this process can reduce the setup time on any piece of equipment by 75 percent without major expense. It doesn't matter whether the machinery is a standard catalog issue or if it is the only one of its kind in the world. Nor does it matter whether the changeover currently takes 24 hours or 12 minutes to accomplish. The challenge and the guarantee stand.

Twice since 1980 I have backed away from issuing that challenge.

The first time was when I ran into a changeover of a process-oriented operation that took 240 hours to complete—24 hours a day for 10 days—during which time the company had to continue to produce the product and throw it away. I decided discretion was the better part of valor and that in all probability I could not guarantee that company a 75 percent reduction without spending a lot of money. As a result we never even started. Today that company avoids changeovers by buying low-volume products from a competitor.

The second time I backed off was with a company that had already reduced a 16-hour changeover to 6½ hours before inviting me in. I was not confident enough to guarantee them a 75 percent reduction on top of the 60 percent they had already accomplished. Together that would have been a 90 percent reduction. Instead I guaranteed them only a reduction from 6½ to 3 hours (54 percent on top of their previous 60 percent, or a total of about 78 percent).

I should have guaranteed the 75 percent even in this case, because the company has been able to reduce the changeover time to under an hour and a half. I underestimated the power of the process and the ability of the people who became the team members for setup reductions, and who generated and implemented the timesaving ideas that made the effort successful.

SETUP REDUCTION GROUND RULES

Let me walk through the setup reduction process that I have found to be so successful. This process starts with a set of ground rules to be agreed upon by management, then entails a specific set of steps.

The ground rules cover three areas, and are stated as questions. The first one is: What is being done? The second is: Why is it being done? The third is: Who is doing it?

Management must agree to, and even sign off on, these ground rules. Some of them are easy to agree to and some of them are not so easy to agree to. Companies that want to reduce setup times for traditional cost reduction purposes will probably not be able to agree to some of these rules. But companies that are reducing setup times within the JIT process will not have trouble with these rules. Once the ground rules are agreed to, they have to stand as the ground rules and guarantees to the people who are doing the setup reduction project.

What Is Being Done?

There are four parts to the definition of *what* setup reduction is about. The first part states that the objective is to simplify setups. It is not to avoid setups. It is not to jump on the forecasting and scheduling people to allow longer runs to avoid setups. The marketplace simply won't allow this anymore. The goal is to simplify the physical act of setting up.

The second part is a measurement of setup time, focusing on machine downtime first and cost second. Cost is important, but the primary focus must be on machine downtime.

Third, the definition of setup time—and it is a strict one—is the time it takes to go from good product to good product. That means the clock starts ticking when the last good piece comes off the machine and it keeps on recording time until that machine is once again up and producing good parts. Teardown, cleanup, putting the new job on, getting it to run right, first-piece inspection, and getting to standard run speed are all included in the setup time for that operation.

Fourth, the objective should be to achieve at least a 75-percent reduction *on a low-cost or no-cost basis.* This could be done in two steps, again using the half-way-to-the-wall idea, first trying to cut setup time by 50 percent, then going for 50 percent again on top of that.

Why Is It Being Done?

The second set of ground rules deals with the issue of why. The first rule is one of the difficult ones and is stated as a negative: Reducing setup is not done to reduce people. This must be agreed to up front by management so it can stand as part of the official ground rules for people involved in the job.

Before JIT most U.S. companies—had they known how to reduce setup times—would have swept through a plant and reduced setup times everywhere by 50 percent, laid off 50 percent of the setup people, and done business as usual. That is exactly the wrong thing to do.

The rule of not reducing people is not a rule for JIT as a whole, just setup reduction. Some companies are implementing JIT for survival, and they must reduce people. But even those companies must agree that setup reduction is not for the purpose of reducing people.

The second rule under why is also difficult and is further complicated by the fact that it is only applicable 90 percent of the time: Reducing setup is not done to produce more. The 10 percent of the time that this does not apply is when a company is turning away business. If a company is not turning away business it must be making enough now. Maybe it is not producing as quickly as it would like, or as efficiently as it would like, but the company is making enough now. Saving an hour of setup time and converting it to one more hour of production would simply put that production in inventory, which is what we want to avoid in the first place.

Why reduce setup time? To reinvest the saved time in more frequent setups so that lot sizes can be reduced. These reduced lot sizes, in turn, help lay the groundwork for JIT, first, by getting a company closer and closer to producing product as frequently as it is required and second, by getting production as smooth and repeatable as possible to develop the balance, synchronization, and flow needed to eliminate waste activities.

But this lot size reduction must be done without incurring any more setup costs than a company now has—no additional machine downtime for setup, no additional material lost (setup scrap), no additional setup people.

Who Is Doing It?

An absolutely vital ground rule of this process is understanding who is involved in it and who has ultimate control. First, reducing setup time is not an engineering project. It is an employee involvement and teamwork project. I don't mean to attack engineers. In fact, I fully realize that in our competition with Japan, the United States does not have enough engineers.

However, for setup reduction, I still believe an engineering approach is the wrong one. Engineers, by training and experience, will tend to concentrate on the mechanics of the changeover—the machine itself or the clamping mechanism for the tool or fixture. The real time consumer in the changeover process, however, is the "administrivia" or "prework" that is now done while the equipment is shut down, as well as the constant problems that interrupt the setup process.

Analysis of what takes the time in changeovers shows that the great majority of total time has nothing to do with the machine or the clamping method. It has to do with organization and timing, such as not being able to find the setup person; or the setup person, when found, not knowing what the next job is; or the setup person finding that the right tools are not in place; or the setup person having to wait for the fork-truck driver. It has to do with things not being done right the first time, such as putting in a tool and finding that it is not sharp, or that it is broken and needs to be fixed, or that fixtures don't have the right length bolts with them.

There is also a tendency among engineers to want to reduce setup times with technology by buying things like rolling bolsters, hydraulic clamping devices, or infrared guard systems. This goes against the low-cost, no-cost ground rule to this effort. The goal is to organize and choreograph things, fix and invent things before buying things.

These are some of the reasons why a pure engineering approach will not work. Far more important, however, are the reasons why an employee involvement/teamwork approach *will* work.

The first reason is that it makes the best use of the real experts—the setup people or operators who know the most about the process and their machines. That is not to say that they are doing everything right now, just that they have the most experience and know the most about today's problems.

The second reason is generating a sense of ownership in the setup reduction process among those people.

The third reason is that bringing more people in brings more resources to bear on problems than if setup reduction is left to engineers.

There is no question that these shop-floor experts probably have at least half the ideas needed to reduce setup time 75 percent already floating around in their heads. Some of these ideas they could talk about today, while others they can't really articulate. But the ideas are there, waiting to be implemented. If there is a need for additional ideas, management should help these experts to generate them, thereby giving them a sense of ownership in the process. After all, they are the ones who will ultimately decide if an idea is good or not and if it will work or not. Once these experts decide that an idea will work, they will overcome any factors hindering implementation of that idea.

If an outsider such as an engineer throws ideas to them, even good ideas, their first reaction will be, "Who is this person? What does he really know about my machine and how to set it up?"

Therefore, these people have to be helped to generate their own ideas, and management must communicate to these shop-floor experts that their ideas not only count, but will be implemented for the betterment of all.

U.S. manufacturers must get beyond the traditional belief that only managers, supervisors, and technical staff have good ideas that can solve problems. There are far too many problems to go around for only managers and technical people to be involved in. All available human resources must be applied to solving problems, especially those individuals who know the most about them.

MAKEUP OF SETUP REDUCTION TEAMS

A typical project team starts with two to four setup people, which makes them physically the largest group in the team. These people would be supported by one or two people from the engineering or technical community.

When a machine is singled out for setup reduction, a company must determine who from the technical community knows most about that piece of equipment. It might be a process engineer. It might be a tool-design engineer. It might be someone from the tool room or from maintenance. It may very well be a combination of all of the above.

It is necessary to point out that engineering, after all, must not lose control of what happens on the shop floor. When an idea generated by the shop-floor experts is determined to be a good one worthy of being pursued, engineers are necessary to make sure that it is implemented with the best possible engineering and tool-design principles, and that any changes to be made will in no way compromise safety or quality requirements. It is vital, however, that these people support rather than dominate. They must be able to ask the right questions and steer the shop-floor experts toward the right answers, rather than throwing their own ideas on the table and defending them to the death.

To round out the team, a team leader (or facilitator) is needed, and, for the first project or two, a guide—someone who has done it before and knows the process.

The team leader, or facilitator, must be able to relate well to the setup people. A facilitator must also have a clear idea of what the management and political processes are within the company, so that turf issues that might otherwise hinder successful implementation can be overcome.

The area supervisor must also be an integral part of the process, although whether he or she is an official team member often depends on his or her individual personality and situation. There are two reasons why supervisors often should not be full-time members of a setup reduction team.

One is that the personality of the supervisor might cause the setup people to sit back and expect the supervisor to take over and be the central focus; this inhibits the setup people from generating ideas.

A second problem supervisors have is that they tend to have the worst attendance records of any member of the team because they are up to their eyeballs in other things all the time. They either cannot attend team meetings or are continually being called out of the meetings. This can be disruptive and can send the wrong signals to the team—that management does not support the effort enough to keep the supervisor in it.

If within a given company these two things are not serious issues, then supervisors should be full-time team members. In instances where supervisors are not full-time team members, the team leaders or facilitators have the added responsibility of keeping the supervisors fully informed and up to date—briefing them after every meeting, inviting them to participate in key meetings, continually getting their help and input, and keeping them part of the process.

Others who are needed periodically—from such functions as cost accounting, finance, production control, engineering in general, or sales and marketing—should be invited on an as-needed basis.

This team should be an action team rather than a study group. If the group is assigned the task of reducing the setup time on a given machine by 75 percent or more, it should be able to go ahead and do it. The group should have a small amount of its own funding—still living within the low-cost, no-cost idea. This money is not for buying solutions, but for getting things done and for experimenting and testing out ideas.

If the group says,"There should be three wheels on this cart instead of four, there should be a toolholder out here, there should be a different storage cabinet," or "We want to try a different method of clamping," the group should be able to get those ideas onto a piece of paper—a sketch, a drawing, a work order—to get something done in the tool room or the metal shop.

The team should always keep its mission in mind, and that mission is to act, not just to study and make recommendations. Because it is an action group, the leader's function is to convert ideas into actions by helping the group decide what the next steps are and who among the team is assigned responsibility for what and by when. The leader will control assignments, make contact with people outside the group, keep things happening between meetings, document progress, and be the team spokesperson.

THE SERIES OF STEPS

The actual setup reduction process entails seven steps. First, management must sign off on all the ground rules. Second, a setup must be chosen, both in terms of the machine and the particular changeover to work on. Third, a team and team leader must be chosen. Fourth, the team must be trained. Fifth, the current actual setup needs to be documented in the form of a videotape. Sixth, the tape must be analyzed in detail by the team. Seventh, ideas for how to make the changeover faster, usually developed during the tape analysis, must be implemented.

Signing off on the ground rules is a self-evident step. As I have mentioned, unless management agrees to and signs off on all the ground rules, the process will not succeed.

When choosing equipment on which to improve the changeover, try to meet two requirements. The first requirement is that there be obvious benefit to the company from reducing the setup time on that particular equipment. The second, equally important, requirement is that the best possible setup people (open-minded, respected by peers) end up on the team.

In choosing the particular changeover to work on, find a changeover that is complex rather than simple, since a complex changeover will usually include all the elements of the simple changeovers.

Choosing teams and team leaders is discussed in detail in the section of the book on management issues.

This portion of the chapter will concentrate on the video-taping and analysis portions of the process.

VIDEOTAPING THE SETUP

Our experience has shown that the best possible way to document and analyze the setup is with videotape. There is no substitute for videotape as a permanent record of what happens for the team to refer back to time after time. Dancers and athletes have been watching videotapes of performances for years. Every Monday during the fall, professional football teams gather to watch the tapes of Sunday's games.

It is hard to get the kind of detail needed through a verbal description of a setup or a formal time-and-motion study.

There is a potential for setup people to misunderstand the purposes of videotaping and to object. Therefore, the ground rules for videotaping must be clear and everyone must understand why the videotape is being made.

One company we worked with provides an extreme example of the kinds of problems some companies have about videotaping. The shop-floor workers had three basic fears.

The first fear was that the time-study department would use it to establish new standards.

The second fear was potential embarrassment, that people would watch the videotape and ridicule them.

The third fear was that the tape would be used to teach others how to set up the equipment. This fear was heightened by rumors that the company was planning to transfer technology and move work to a plant out of the country.

To demonstrate that these fears were groundless, we offered to make the tape the exclusive property of the team. Somebody from the team would be present when the setup was taped and would take possession of the tape immediately. The team would decide when and to whom the tape would be shown. After each team meeting, the tape would be given to a team member to put in a lockup or to take home.

It took only two weeks of meetings for the team (and their fellow shop-floor employees) to understand the true reason for the tape being made and the tape's usefulness, and for these rules to be relaxed.

In other instances it has been enough to invite the union president or a representative to sit in on team meetings as an observer until he or she is satisfied that the process is in the best interests of all parties. It has never taken more than two meetings for the union representative to be satisfied.

It is not easy to get a real-life videotape. The most obvious problem is caused by the so-called Heisenberg principle, named for a German physicist—the idea that a phenomenon that is observed is changed merely by the fact that it is being observed.

The most common change we run into is that people's pride

gets in the way and they treat the taping as an Olympic event. They do preparation that would not normally be done. They cut corners. This defeats the purpose and does not give the team a true picture of the length of time involved and the problems that are encountered all the time in setup.

There are some techniques that minimize this effect.

One is to do practice runs. Practice runs have the dual effect of getting people used to being videotaped and providing a learning experience for the people taping as to angle, light, and distance.

A second technique is not to announce which changeover will be videotaped. The camera should be brought out and set up before the previous job is finished running, leaving no time for special preparations.

The ideal videotape would show the last good piece from the previous job coming off the machine. Then the clock would immediately start for changeover and the videotape would continue to register everything from that point on.

Once there is a videotape, the next step is to start the team meetings and analyze the tape. Typically there is a flurry of meetings at the beginning—for training in team building, getting to know each other, getting to know personal styles of analysis, risk taking, and other issues. Then the group spends a few meetings analyzing the tape in great detail and generating a list of problems to solve and ideas to pursue. After that, most groups settle into a routine of a meeting a week.

SETUP ANALYSIS

In analyzing the videotape, the team looks for four types of activity:

Internal–external
Adjustments
Clamping
Problems

Internal–External

In this step each activity in the videotape is labeled as an internal activity or an external activity. Internal work is defined as work that can only be done when the equipment is stopped. External work is defined as work that is being done when the equipment is stopped, although there is no technical reason why the machine has to be stopped.

We then apply a rule that says: Any activity that can be done with the machine running (and producing) will be done with the machine running—we will find a way.

There will be obvious external activities, such as somebody asking what the next job is, finding the correct fixtures, or going to the tool crib to get the tools.

There will also be less obvious external activities such as cleaning and putting away parts or fixtures from the previous job, or leaving the machine because a collet has been borrowed, a clamp doesn't have the proper length bolts, or a tool is not sharp. All of these are classified as external, and would be identified as something to be done either ahead of time or after the machine is up and running.

This analysis of external activities does not necessarily reduce the amount of work to be done, but instead changes the timing of when the work is done in order to reduce machine downtime. Remember the ground rule—cost is important but the primary focus must be on machine downtime.

Once this rule has been successfully applied, only purely internal activities are left—activities that can only be done with the machine stopped. The next goal is to try to convert some internal activities to external activities so they can be done with the equipment running.

An obvious example of converting an internal activity to an external one is the presetting of tools for numerically controlled equipment. It used to be that the setting of the tools in the toolholders was only done during setup with the machine stopped. Now it is done off-line ahead of time.

Adjustments

A second major category to be examined is adjustments. There are four or five different things to look for under adjustments, and the goal is to eliminate adjustments of any kind.

First of all, it very often takes a short period of time to get the old job off and the new job on, but a long period of time to get things to run right. All that time is adjustment. A part is run through, only to find that it is not good. An adjustment is made and another part is run through to see if it is any better. This one-at-a-time production and inspection continues until good product is being made.

In our setup reduction program, that practice is taboo. There should never be a part spoiled during the setup. In a perfect world, the first part would always be right.

For a second type of adjustment, think of a press. It may take a short period of time to get a die onto the bed of a press but much longer to get the die in exactly the right position (squared, centered, etc.) to be ready for clamping. That is all adjustment. We want the first motion of getting the die onto the bed to be the only one necessary, that is—for the die to be self-positioning.

A third type of adjustment is due to the fact that most equipment is designed to be infinitely adjustable over a given range. A person loosens something, moves it to a new spot, measures it, tinkers with it a little bit, and clamps it down.

Machines are designed to be infinitely adjustable because no one knows exactly what they will be used for. If we look at how a particular piece of equipment is being used, it may be that only a small number of those positions are needed. If so, it is possible to convert to positive stops rather than measured infinite adjustment. We can use a wide variety of mechanisms, such as stops, dogs, slots, notches, or spring-loaded pins, and a set of instructions that say to make Part A, B, or F, move to Slot 4.

Another adjustment problem is that there are often several different ways to accomplish a given adjustment. It is an eternal truth that, if something can be adjusted, sooner or later someone will adjust it. One of the techniques we use is to establish a permanent home-base position for some of these adjustments and never move them again during changeover or production.

Clamping

A third major category is clamping. If the videotape shows that a lot of time is spent loosening, tightening, clamping, and unclamping, we will look at clamping methods.

North American engineers only seem to know one method of holding things together—bolts. And if there is enough room, the magic number seems to be 16 bolts to do it right. That is probably enough holding power to overcome 30,000 pounds of force.

I have become almost fanatical in my dislike for threads—bolts, nuts, and screws—when it comes to changeover.

I have only two good things to say about threads. They have tremendous holding power, and they do not take up much room to do their holding. This makes threads ideal for permanent positions. But for changeovers they are about as inefficient a method as anyone could invent.

Think about threads. Putting a bolt into a threaded hole or a nut onto a bolt is a very precise operation. If it is not done gently and exactly, the result will be crossed threads and problems or even damage. Dirt gets into threads, threads freeze up, threads strip out.

Tools are needed with threads—and we all know what happens with tools. Tools get lost, tools get dropped, tools get stolen, tools get borrowed, tools are not where they are supposed to be. Tools slip and cause bloodied knuckles. Tools are too long and won't go far enough around so we take them off and put them on, take them off and put them on. Tools are too short and don't give enough leverage without a cheater—another tool. Bolts break. One of the 16 bolts gets replaced and, lo and behold, it has a different head size. Now another tool is needed.

Also, it is only the last half turn of a bolt, nut, or screw that actually does the job. How often does it take 20 turns (or 40 half turns) simply to get to the last half turn that matters? And in reverse, it is the first half turn that loosens.

If the videotape tells us that a significant amount of time is spent clamping and unclamping, we look for alternative methods. First we examine the forces involved. What is the downward force, upward force, side-to-side force, torquing force? How much force must be overcome? What methods, other than threads, are there to overcome this force?

There are levers, cam-action clamps, gibs, pins, wedges, and any number of other methods. In selecting another method we look to accomplish two goals:

Eliminate tools.

Find a method that requires only one or, at most, two motions.

Problems

The fourth area, problems, is a catchall for anything that would stand in the way of a perfect, trouble-free, uninterrupted setup. These problems are usually the dozens of little problems that aren't even seen anymore. People have lived with them so long that they have become a part of the way of doing business.

It is not enough to look for ways to make the setup easier in spite of problems, but rather for ways to prevent the problem from happening in the first place.

The most powerful technique to use to get to root causes of these problems is to ask the question: Why? The question must be asked not once, but four or five times, each time peeling the problem back one more layer and getting closer to the ultimate cause.

People get angry and defensive when they are asked Why? Why? Why? Why? Why? The best way to prevent people from getting angry and defensive is by telling them ahead of time that this is the technique we use, even trying to make a game of it; asking why, and answering just the first layer of the question;

only to ask why again, and trying to get the next answer to go a layer deeper.

Many people learn, ultimately, not to underestimate the power of asking why in all areas of the business. Amazing things happen when companies question any and all current practices.

It should be clear that reducing setup time is a vital first step if other aspects of Just In Time are to be implemented.

Reducing setup time is far easier and cheaper than anyone would think before they have personally used this procedure. Remember, it only takes stubbornness to get 75 percent reduction in setup time on a low-cost or no-cost basis.

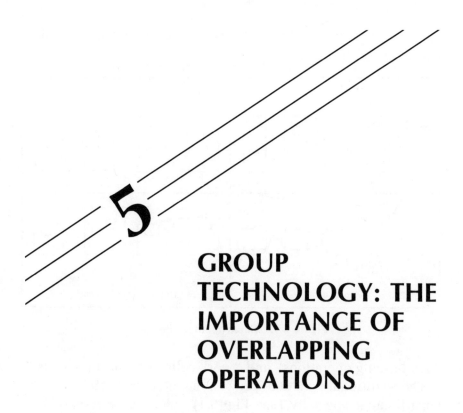

GROUP TECHNOLOGY: THE IMPORTANCE OF OVERLAPPING OPERATIONS

The term "group technology" is commonly used when people think about the physical layout, arrangement, and location of machinery in a manufacturing plant. This is a sophisticated term that comes to us primarily from European industry, and it conjures up images of special coding and unique computer software capable of sorting out thousands of different parts and components into logical product groups or families.

The Just In Time use of the term "group technology" is much less complex than this. A more suitable definition of group technology, for the kind of physical layout and arrangement of machines that Just In Time calls for, would include the words

71

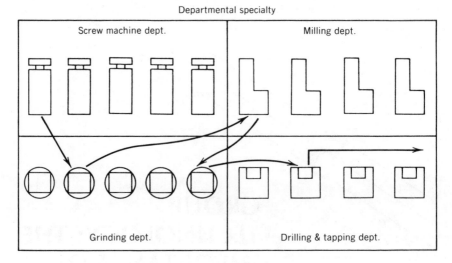

Figure 5.1. Departmental Specialty

"overlapping operations" and "work cells" or "machine cells."

The traditional way to organize a manufacturing facility is by departmental specialty (see Fig. 5.1), where each department specializes in a type of equipment or technology. All the screw machines are in one department, all the grinders in another department, milling is done in another area, and drilling and tapping is in yet another area. Again, this is a metalworking example, but the same situation holds true in electronics, pharmaceuticals, textiles, food—in fact, in virtually all industries.

When factories are laid out and arranged by functional departments, the company inevitably ends up producing product in batches. Operation 1 is usually completed for an entire batch before that batch is moved to operation 2. This is exactly opposite to the way Just In Time asks that goods be produced. (See Fig. 5.2.)

First and foremost, Just In Time asks that the facility be physically laid out by product rather than by function. The equipment is dedicated or semidedicated to a family of products and arranged in the order in which operations are to be performed on that family of products.

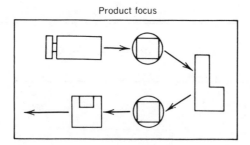

Figure 5.2. The Just-In-Time Way to Produce Goods

TRUE JUST-IN-TIME WORK CELLS

The terms "group technology" and "machine cell" are older than JIT. JIT puts very strict limitations on what is a proper machine cell. In most instances, what has been organized in the past and called a machine cell does not meet JIT requirements.

There are two tests that can be performed to see if a true JIT cell exists.

The first test is whether the product is flowing one at a time from machine to machine. Many older versions of machine cells did not pass this test. True, the equipment was dedicated and put physically together, but the product often still moved in batches from one operation to the next.

Absolute insistence on one-at-a-time manufacturing is consistent with our recurring theme of Henry Ford's assembly line (see Fig. 5.3), in this case applying assembly line principles to fabricating or machining operations.

This one-at-a-time flow is what creates overlapping operations. It creates a flow whereby operation 2 is started as soon as the very first part comes out of operation 1. In effect, the "batch" becomes one piece.

The second test to see if a machine cell is truly a JIT cell is whether the machine cell has the flexibility to be operated at different output rates and with different crew sizes (cycle time).

Traditional machine cells have rarely been concerned with

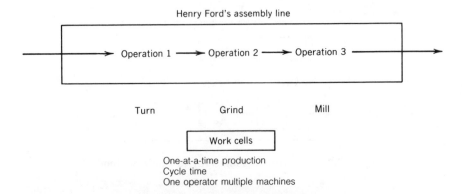

Figure 5.3. Henry Ford's Assembly Line

flexibility. They have been laid out and manned at essentially one output level—the maximum per hour that the equipment can produce.

It is necessary for Just-In-Time work cells to be adjustable to be able to produce at the rate required by whatever operation or customer it is feeding, recognizing that the customer will be adjusting his hypothetical rheostat each month.

Once a JIT work cell has been established, two questions need to be asked:

1. What is needed from this work cell for this particular production period?
2. How many operators are needed in that work cell in order to get exactly the amount of product that is needed?

Note that neither question is the traditional one: How fast can this work cell produce?

If this work cell, for instance, produces a component for the assembly line that we spoke about in Chapter 3, the answer to the question What is needed from this work cell in this period? would be one part every 18 seconds.

The next step would be to determine how many operators are needed to produce one every 18 seconds.

MULTIPLE MACHINES

By first asking what is needed, and then asking how many operators are needed in a particular month to meet that month's production requirements, we establish the Just-In-Time concept of
"one operator, multiple machines."

Again, on the surface this doesn't sound very different from
traditional manufacturing. There are many companies in the
United States today that have one operator responsible for more
than one machine. However, in most cases, the practice is for the
one operator to be running two, three, or four similar machines,
and usually each machine is making a different part.

In a Just-In-Time work cell, one operator runs two, three, or
four different machines, all performing operations on the same
part, moving that part from operation to operation in sequence
one at a time.

One of the most frequently asked questions about work cells in
Just In Time is whether setting up work cells necessitates dedicating machines. In theory the answer is yes—a machine in a
work cell is dedicated to that cell. But in reality, there are ways
to get around having machinery locked into a machine cell if that
would necessitate purchasing additional machines to do other
work.

One way to get around this problem is to semi-dedicate the
equipment to a work cell. This would mean physically placing
that machine into a work cell, but running the equipment as a
work cell only part of the day. During the other part of each day
the machines can be scheduled independently, as if they were
not in a work cell.

A second way to maintain equipment flexibility is to create
temporary work cells, to be put together for specific or sporadic
requirements, then taken apart again when the requirements are
satisfied.

Obviously, this would be practical only with relatively small
and easily moved equipment.

When there are truly not enough machines to go around, it is possible to use another JIT technique—a pull system, or linking operations (Chapter 6), to make it seem that one machine is in two or three cells.

OPERATOR IN MOTION

When an operator is moving product one at a time from operation to operation, the operator is necessarily in motion (see Figure 5.4). A number of benefits accrue when the concept of an operator in motion is introduced. One is improvements in health and mental alertness.

A common practice is to have operators sitting down. Yet studies show that it is better for operators' health and mental alertness to stand—even better if the operator can take a step or two. Mental alertness has an effect on safety and product quality.

In addition, if an operator is sitting down, he can only reach things within a small area. Standing, the operator has a greater reach. With the ability to move a step or two in each direction, the operator has far greater reach. Since the stepping and reaching are simultaneous the flexibility gains incur no loss of time.

There are other benefits to having an operator in motion.

In the typical batch environment, an operator is paid to put

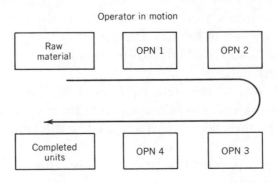

Figure 5.4.   Operator in Motion

material into a container after each operation. When the container is full or the lot is finished, a fork-truck driver is paid to move it to another part of the plant for the next operation. Then another operator is paid to take it out of a container and put it into the next operation.

In a JIT work cell, the operator takes the material out of the first machine and puts it directly into the next machine. There is no fork truck, and people are no longer paid to put material into or take material out of containers.

Another major benefit—something that happens for free—is that each successive operation often constitutes a 100 percent inspection of the previous operation, eliminating the need to pay someone to perform a separate inspection operation.

FLEXIBLE LAYOUT

As I stressed in Chapter 3, the key to being able to implement cycle time is being able to flex the crew size. In turn, there are two keys to being able to flex the crew size without paying a penalty in lost efficiency (cost). One of those keys, flexibility of the work force, was discussed in Chapter 3. The other key is a specific, flexible layout.

U-LINE LAYOUTS

The principle of flexible layout applies equally well to reengineering assembly lines and to work cells being put together out of operations that have never before been together.

Figure 5.5 is probably the best-known example of this type of layout—the U-line.

The magic of the U-line layout is not in the U shape, but in the fact that the operators are physically together—side by side, back to back. They are not so close that they are annoying or hindering each other. But they are physically together, with no barriers be-

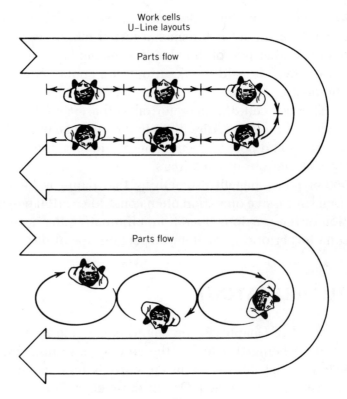

Work cells
U–Line layouts

Parts flow

Parts flow

Figure 5.5.   Work Cells: U-Line Layouts

tween them. All the work to be done in this line or cell is available to be done from one limited central area. In this way, the number of operators needed to do that job is flexible.

Each production period, the question can be asked again: How many operators need to be put in this limited central area to get the necessary output? In this line, if one month the output equivalent of six operators is needed and the next month the output of only three operators is needed because of a change in requirements, then three people can be put into that same layout to do the work, because it is all available from a central area. The idea is to give each person in the cell the opportunity to reach as much work as possible.

In a straight line the task of dividing the work of six operators into three is difficult. With operators working only side-by-side, the only option would be for operator 1 to do the work of operators 1 and 2. But then, he or she would be walking back empty-handed to start the next cycle. That would be inefficient.

If the layout allows operators to be back-to-back as well, a better option exists. One operator can do operation 1 then turn around and do operation 6.

Too few people think outside the traditional engineering book for alternatives in manning. Most people don't realize the effectiveness of working back-to-back. If an operator doesn't have a full work load with one operation, most people naturally think to have the operator go to the next operation either up or down in sequence.

In a U-line, operators are not limited to the next operation up or down the line. Because they have 360-degree mobility, they can take on all or part of any job that is within reach in a full circle.

Figure 5.6 shows a different arrangement that accomplishes the same degree of flexibility as the U-line. It is made up of two straight lines laid out back-to-back, in this case with opposing flow directions. Again, the people are physically together, side-by-side and back-to-back. The people on each line have a similar circular range of motion as they do on a U-line.

The lines may make similar parts or they may be totally unrelated. Often, unrelated lines or jobs are put together in order to group people for flexibility. If there is just a single person running a work cell, that does not afford a great deal of flexibility to increase or decrease the output in small increments—by 20 percent for instance. The only options are to add another operator (increasing output by 100 percent), or shut the machine off (decreasing output by 100 percent). In order to get any significant flexibility, a crew must have five or six people, even if that means artificially grouping jobs to create a larger crew.

Neither of these is the typical layout I see when I go to plants.

The most common layout in manufacturing today, whether it is an assembly line or a traditional machine cell, is a long,

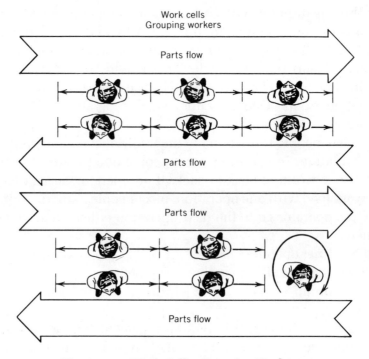

Figure 5.6.   Work Cells: Grouping Workers

straight line with the operators spread out. Spreading operators out creates space barriers between operators and, in effect, spreads the work out.

People are staggered on different sides of the line. In such a case, the line itself becomes a barrier physically separating people. A machine is put between people. Stock boxes and work benches are put between people. In short, not only are the people spread out, but they are physically isolated from one another. In such a layout, if next month the output of one less operator is needed, it is impossible to eliminate that operator. The work has been parceled into a fixed number of separate areas and there must be a person in each of those areas or the line or cell won't run. This is not flexible.

LAYOUT AND WORK CELLS—A CASE STUDY

I worked with a company on an assignment where I visited once a month for two days. They were not in the process of a major implementation of Just In Time. Rather, we were experimenting with a number of different JIT techniques. We had done some setup reduction, a pull system, and other things. They then wanted to get into work cells. The company was traditionally oriented in that it had all its milling in one department, drilling and tapping in another department, and so forth. They wanted the best way to start learning about how to put work cells together under Just In Time.

I knew their operation well enough to advise them that even though there were departmental specialties, there were also a lot of machines that were dedicated to specific parts or families of parts. I suggested they look for examples of parts where four of five operations in a row were already made on equipment dedicated to that part or family of parts.

That is the easiest way to get started, not to have to worry about such things as competing for capacity.

I went away for a month thinking that probably all they would do would be to identify these pieces of equipment and that when I returned on my next visit we would talk about the next steps, which would be to pick the machines up and relocate them, put them together in a new layout, and so forth. But this was a fast-moving, aggressive company. They went much further than I expected and in a short period of time actually had three work cells operating after a fashion.

When I returned a month later, some people met me on the front steps of the factory.

They had good news. But they also had problems. They needed help.

The first part of the good news was that material handling requirements had been reduced so much by the three work cells that the company had put a fork truck up for sale. The second part of the good news was specific to one of the work cells they had put together.

I was taken out to the floor to that work cell and shown how it was operating.

The company realized that when the machines were separated in different departments there was a three-week lead time to get parts through these operations. The way this was discovered was that when people went to pick up the machines to put them into a work cell they found three weeks of work-in-process inventory. With the work cells there would be much less but they didn't know yet exactly how much less.

The work cell I was shown (Figure 5.7) started with three ma-

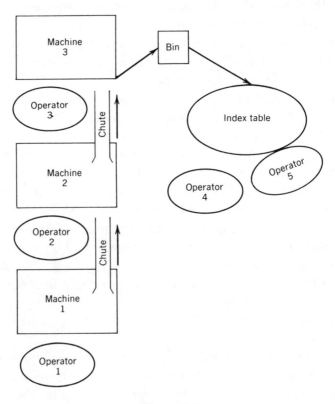

Figure 5.7.

chines, each with an operator. Parts were going down a chute from the first machine to the second, and down another chute from the second machine to the third. At the third machine the parts were accumulated in a bin. When the bin was full, it was moved to a fourth machine, an index table. The index table was off to the side with one operator doing an assembly operation and another doing 100 percent inspection.

The first part of the bad news was the cost accounting department. Cost accounting was complaining that costs were going crazy. A machine had been taken out of Department 1, where there was an overhead rate of 320 percent. Another machine was taken from Department 6, with an overhead rate of 480 precent. These machines, and two others, were put in an area with an overhead rate of 800 percent. Cost accounting was afraid the operation would lose money.

Of course, that was really not a problem I had to deal with. I refuse to take seriously a statement that says if a machine is picked up and moved a few hundred feet, costs change. The shop floor simply needed to educate cost accounting. But they wanted me to know about it.

The real problem, they said, was balance. As shown in Figure 5.8, the first two machines produced at 700 per hour, the third at 600 per hour and the fourth at 450 per hour. The operators of the first two machines were getting along very well, but the operator of the third machine was working as fast as she could, constantly looking over her shoulder as inventory piled up behind her. She, in turn, was overwhelming the fourth machine. They needed to know what to balance to.

The answer, of course, is cycle time.

The foreman went off that night to reread the booklet on cycle time.

He came back the next day, having determined that he needed 20,000 parts per week, and that the best way to do that was to run the equipment in two shifts. According to the principle of cycle time, that meant producing 250 parts per hour, or, to be safe, 300 parts per hour—one every 12 seconds. Slowing the index table

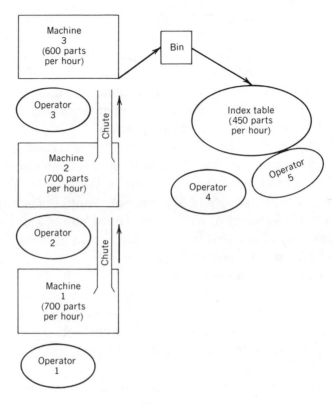

Figure 5.8.

down to 300 parts per hour meant that one operator could easily do both the assembly and inspection in 12 seconds.

The next step was to put the other three machines together in a U shape, and slow them down to 300 parts per hour as well. But one operator could not quite do all three operations in 12 seconds.

In addition, the index table was still far away from the other three machines. I suggested they move the index table as close as possible to the other three machines, and position the operator centrally within the work cell (Figure 5.9). The work on the index table was still easy, so the index table operator could help herself to her parts by taking them from the third machine, re-

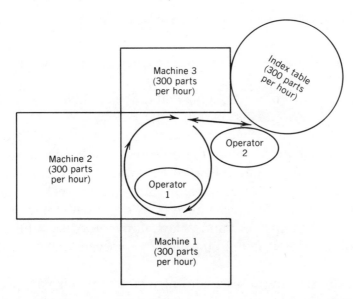

Figure 5.9.

ducing the first operator's work, which made it possible for the first operator to complete all the other tasks in 12 seconds.

The final step was to make sure there was cooperation. If the two operators were both flexible, they could switch off from the easy job to the difficult one every so often.

I went away for a month. When I came back, people were waiting for me again with the same story—good news and bad news.

The good news: In the month the work cell had been running, quality problems and costs had gone down by about 80 percent. Previously, quality problems from operation 1 were often not caught until the index table procedure three weeks later, when there were already 20,000 to 60,000 parts in process that had to be sorted, reworked, or perhaps scrapped.

Now such quality problems were being found 24 seconds later and there was no longer an inventory of 60,000 suspect parts, but only two or three at the most.

There was more good news. Lead time for a product dropped

from three weeks to 24 seconds. Actually, this is a numbers game. The lead time was really one week—the time it took to make a week's worth. But there was even more good news with respect to lead time and its impact on inventory. Inventory at any given time was now averaging half a week (10,000 parts) instead of three weeks (60,000 parts).

More good news had come in the form of a request from the company's main customer to implement Just In Time and ship a day's worth every day. The company was already producing every day, although it was only shipping once a week, so the purchaser, in effect, had just agreed to take another chunk of inventory off the company's hands. Now, if inventory is counted at the end of any day it is not 60,000 parts, or even 10,000 parts, but zero.

The purchasing and scheduling people were also happy. They no longer had to supply 20,000 blanks every Monday morning. The purchasing department now had flexibility to bring in a day's worth every day provided they could find an economical way to do so.

There was, however, some bad news as well. Some manufacturing people had doubts about the cell's efficiency. For example, the manager of Department 1, which used to own the first machine, was prowling around muttering, "When I owned that machine, I produced 700 per hour. You're only producing 300 per hour. That seems wasteful."

When people were asked if they were getting everything they needed from the machine, the grudging answer was yes. They were still uncomfortable because the machine was not running as fast as it could. As with many people who have a traditional manufacturing mindset, they had trouble thinking about producing at the requirement rate rather than the machine rate.

The manufacturing people also worried that with equipment dependent on one another for one-at-a-time production, if one machine broke down the whole cell would have to be shut down.

Indeed, that is really not bad news at all—it is part of the philosophy of Just In Time. If a machine breaks down, the problem should be permanently solved. Under the traditional Western manufacturing system, problems are buffered with inventory and not really solved. The machine is "band-aided" only to break down again.

Now, most people think shutting the line down is the worst thing that can be done. But, in reality, stopping the line is only the third worst thing that can happen.

The worst thing that can happen is to make another defective part.

The second worst thing is to allow a problem to happen, such as a breakdown, and not use that as an opportunity to solve the problem permanently.

If it takes the third worst thing in the world to create enough pain to focus management and technical attention on the two worse things, then that is what JIT will do—force permanent solving of problems.

Cost Accounting and Standards

There was more bad news. It came from cost accounting again. The cost accounting people threatened to send out unfavorable variances because the machine cell was making 300 pieces per hour with a machine that had a frozen standard of 700 pieces per hour. We had to convince them that their system of measurement and standards was what needed to be examined, not the variances of the work cell.

We gave them a quick seminar on Just In Time, then took them out to the work cell. We told them we would give them a good argument why the unit using the work cell should actually get favorable variances. It was a six-part argument.

First, a fork truck had been sold. Second, the cost of quality had gone down by 80 percent on the part being manufactured. Third, manufacturing lead time had gone from three weeks to 24 seconds. Fourth, work-in-process inventory had gone down from 60,000 parts to zero. Fifth, purchased material inventories were going down, probably by about 80 percent. Sixth, add up the labor content of the original standard—two people doing operations at 700 per hour, one at 600 per hour and two at 450 per hour. Then compare that to the new method of two people doing all operations at 300 per hour, and it can be seen that direct labor content per piece is down by more than 25 percent.

I warned them not to send anyone unfavorable variances of any kind! Nothing was unfavorable; everything was favorable!

This example shows as clearly as anything that JIT is not a new set of trade-offs. If done properly, JIT never causes anything to get worse. Everything gets better.

VALUE-ADDED ANALYSIS

Here is a real-life example of a work cell recently put together by a company in the automotive after-market business. The cell includes machining operations, as well as assembly, testing, and packing operations.

This work cell was put together by a successful company, one that had a piecework incentive program that was well conceived and tightly controlled. Because of this, some people were very skeptical that improvements could be made in direct labor, and in fact were worried that changes we might make by instituting a work cell would actually hurt efficiency in terms of direct labor.

But the company had the courage to experiment, and the results were truly amazing.

We started by making a detailed value-added chart (Exhibits 5-1 and 5-2), which showed that out of 187 steps, only 13—about 7 percent—truly added value.

Of the 146 original steps to this point in the process, 108 steps were eliminated directly because of the organization of a work cell and the one-at-a-time production in that work cell. (See Exhibit 5-3.)

Because the work cell reduced throughput time drastically (see Exhibit 5-4), product was no longer manufactured to forecast

EXHIBIT 5-1

	Activity	Adds Value	Distance Traveled (feet)
1.	Unload from truck		20
2.	Wait on dock		
3.	Move to scale		100
4.	Weigh		
5.	Move to storage		50
6.	Store		
7.	Move to double-end operation		325
8.	Store in Q		
9.	Double end	X	10
10.	Aside to tray on conveyor		2
11.	Wait		
12.	Move to gundrill		30
13.	Wait		
14.	Pieces to workplace		5
15.	Wait		
16.	Gundrill	X	1
17.	Aside 90° to workplace		3
18.	Roll burnish	X	1
19.	Aside 90° to tray on conveyor		3
20.	Wait		
21.	Move to 1st Scholin		12
22.	Wait		
23.	Drill and tap inlet hole	X	10
24.	Aside to tray on conveyor		3
25.	Move to 2nd Scholin		12

EXHIBIT 5-1 (continued)

	Activity	Adds Value	Distance Traveled (feet)
26.	Wait		
27.	Drill and tap bleeder hole	X	10
28.	Aside to tray on roller stand		3
29.	Wait		
30.	Move to temporary storage		15
31.	Store		
32.	Move to staging at washer		190
33.	Wait		
34.	Move to work area		15
35.	Wait		
36.	Move pieces to brush table ($\pm 150 = 2$ layers)		5
37.	Wait		
38.	Aside layer separators		10
39.	Brush to remove dirt and chips (1st)		3
40.	Aside to conveyor		1
41.	Wait		
42.	Brush to clean (2nd)		1
43.	Aside to conveyor		1
44.	Convey through washer		50
45.	Wait		
46.	100% inspect		2
47.	Aside to small box		1
48.	Wait		
49.	Small boxful to container on floor		10

EXHIBIT 5-1 (continued)

Activity	Adds Value	Distance Traveled (feet)
50. Wait to fill container (1st layer = ±500 pieces)		
51. Get and place separator between layers		
52. Wait to fill container (2nd layer = ±500 pieces)		
53. Wait for trucker		
54. Move to temporary storage		20
55. Store		
56. Make up and attach production move ticket		
57. Wait		
58. Move to trolley loader		25
59. Wait		
60. Place on loader		5
61. Wait for trolley		
62. Place container on trolley		5
63. Move on trolley to conveyor		80
64. Place on conveyor		5
65. Wait Delays for full conveyor Interference from other components		
66. Move to bulk storage entrance		90
67. Wait		
68. Pick up containerful with FLT		

EXHIBIT 5-1 (continued)

	Activity	Adds Value	Distance Traveled (feet)
69.	Move to aisle		15
70.	Place in aisle		
71.	Return to conveyor		15
72.	Pick up 2nd containerful		
73.	Move to 1st containerful		15
74.	Place on 1st containerful		
75.	Pick up both containers		
76.	Move to bulk storage (midpoint)		95
77.	Place in storage		15
78.	Store		
79.	Get containerful		15
80.	Move to assembly staging		250
81.	Store		
82.	Move to work area		80
83.	Wait		
84.	Fill tub with ±40 pieces		1
85.	Tub to workplace and dump into bin		6
86.	Wait		
87.	Assemble bleed screw	X	1
88.	Aside to tray		1
89.	Wait		
90.	Trayful to assemble insert		3
91.	Wait		
92.	Assemble insert	X	1
93.	Aside to tray		1

EXHIBIT 5-1 (continued)

	Activity	Adds Value	Distance Traveled (feet)
94.	Wait		
95.	Aside trayful to container on roll stand		4
96.	Wait		
97.	Move to staging		30
98.	Store		
99.	Move to assembly workplace		60
100.	Wait in Q		
101.	Move pieces to workbench		6
102.	Wait in Q		
103.	1st assembly	X	3
104.	Aside to bench		1
105.	Wait in Q		
106.	Move pieces to 2nd assembly		2
107.	Wait in Q		
108.	2nd assembly	X	3
109.	Aside to tray (OWOSU = one way, one side up)		4
110.	Wait in Q		
111.	Move to test		4
112.	Wait in Q		
113.	Test		2
114.	Aside to workplace		1
115.	Wait in Q		
116.	Aside to container (OWOSU) in layers		5

EXHIBIT 5-1 (continued)

	Activity	Adds Value	Distance Traveled (feet)
117.	Wait		
118.	Place separators between layers		
119.	Wait		
120.	Move to bulk storage		150
121.	Place in storage		15
122.	Store		
123.	Get containerful		15
124.	Move to packing area		150
125.	Store		
126.	Move to end of packing line		30
127.	Wait		
128.	Move to conveyor		10
129.	Wait		
130.	Place on conveyor		5
131.	Move to work place		10
132.	Wait		
133.	Pack one per box	X	2
134.	Place on packing conveyor		1
135.	Convey through printer to table (print box end)	X	15
136.	Wait on table		
137.	Pack in carton (10 or 20)	X	1
138.	Wait to fill carton		
139.	Place carton on tape conveyor		1

EXHIBIT 5-1 (continued)

Activity	Adds Value	Distance Traveled (feet)
140. Tape box	X	2
141. Wait		
142. Move to roller conveyor		1
143. Convey to table		15
144. Wait on table		
145. Move carton to pallet		6
146. Touchup printing with marking pen		
147. Wait to fill pallet		
148. Move to staging		30
149. Wait		
150. Move pallet load to scales		100
151. Place on scales		5
152. Weigh		
153. Remove from scales		5
154. Pallet load to bulk storage		150
155. Place in storage		15
156. Store		
157. Get pallet load		15
158. Move to check station #3		325
159. Wait in Q		
160. Paperwork		
161. Wait		
162. Move to FG storage		215
163. Place in rack levels 3-4-5		18
164. Store		
165. Get pallet load		18

EXHIBIT 5-1 (continued)

Activity	Adds Value	Distance Traveled (feet)
166. Place in rack levels 1-2		6
167. Store		
168. Pick order to skid		75
169. Wait to fill skid		
170. Move skid to staging		80
171. Wait to pick order		
172. Check count		
173. Stencil boxes		
174. Wait		
175. Move order to shipping staging		80
176. Wait		
177. Move order to stretch wrap		50
178. Wait		
179. Stretch wrap		20
180. Wait to complete stretch wrap		
181. Move to shipping dock		50
182. Wait		
183. Stage order		20
184. Wait to complete staging order		
185. Load on truck		40
186. Wait to load order		
187. Ship		

EXHIBIT 5-2
Summary

	Number	% of Total
Value-added activities	13	7
Move	88	47
Wait/store	69	37
Other	17	9
Total Activities	187	100

Distance traveled	3,519 feet
Work-in-process inventory	11,500 pieces
Throughput time	
Normal	4–6 weeks
Expedited	2 weeks

After setting up the machine cell, the process looked like Exhibit 5-3.

EXHIBIT 5-3

	Activity	Adds Value	Distance Traveled (feet)
1.	Unload from truck		20
2.	Wait on dock		
3.	Move to scale		100
4.	Weigh		
5.	Move to storage		50
6.	Storage		
7.	Move to double-end operation		325

97

EXHIBIT 5-3 (continued)

Activity	Adds Value	Distance Traveled (feet)
8. Store in Q		
9. Double end	X	10
10–15 (Out)		
16. Gundrill	X	1
17. Aside 90 degrees to workplace		3
18. Roll burnish	X	1
19–22 (Out)		
23. Drill and tap inlet hole	X	1
24–26 (Out)		
27. Drill and tap bleeder hole	X	2
28. Wash		3
29–86 (Out)		
87. Assemble bleed screw	X	1
88–91 (Out)		
92. Assemble insert	X	1
93–102 (Out)		
103. 1st assembly	X	3
104–107 (Out)		
108. 2nd assembly	X	3
109. Aside to tray		4
110. Wait in Q		
111. Move to test		4
112. Wait in Q		
113. Test		2
114–132 (Out)		

EXHIBIT 5-3 (continued)

Activity	Adds Value	Distance Traveled (feet)
133. Pack one per box	X	2
134. Place on packing conveyor		1
135. Convey through printer to table (print box end)	X	15
136. Wait on table		
137. Pack in carton (10 or 20)	X	1
138. Wait to fill carton		
139. Place carton on tape conveyor		1
140. Tape box	X	2
141. Wait		
142. Move to roller conveyor		1
143. Convey to table		15
144. Wait on table		
145. Move carton to pallet		6
146. Touch up printing with marking pen		
147–168 (Out)		
169. Wait to fill skid		
170. Move skid to staging		80
171. Wait to pick order		
172. Check count		
173. Stencil boxes		
174. Wait		
175. Move order to shipping staging		80
176. Wait		

EXHIBIT 5-3 (continued)

Activity	Adds Value	Distance Traveled (feet)
177. Move order to stretch wrap		50
178. Wait		
179. Stretch wrap		20
180. Wait to complete stretch wrap		
181. Move to shipping dock		50
182. Wait		
183. Stage order		20
184. Wait to complete staging order		
185. Load on truck		40
186. Wait to load order		
187. Ship		

EXHIBIT 5-4
Summary (Before and After)

	Before	After	Improvement
Value added activities	13	13	—
Move	88	11	88%
Wait/store	69	18	74%
Other	17	15	12%
Total activities	187	57	70%
Distance traveled	3,519 feet	618 feet	82%
WIP inventory	11,500 pieces	11 pieces	99%+

EXHIBIT 5-4 (continued)

	Before	After	Improvement
Throughput time			
Normal	4–6 weeks	2.4 minutes	99% +
Expedited	2 weeks	2.4 minutes	99% +

but to specific customer orders and another 22 steps were able to come out of the storage and order picking process.

Reductions in the number of process steps, distance traveled, inventory, and throughput time were not the only significant benefits. Direct labor was reduced 36 percent by the simplification of methods (almost automatic with one-at-a-time processing) and by finding that two operations (brush/wash and inspect/pack) were no longer needed at all. Indirect labor, except for receiving and shipping, was eliminated completely.

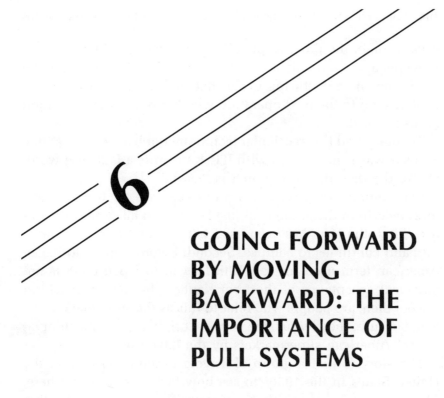

GOING FORWARD BY MOVING BACKWARD: THE IMPORTANCE OF PULL SYSTEMS

In Chapter 5 we saw the concept of overlapping operations, the ideal way to perform a series of operations on a product. In a perfect JIT world, families of products would be produced in machine cells and would move from operation to operation. In reality there will be many instances where we cannot yet solve the problems necessary to get to perfect one-at-a-time production but must continue to produce in batches. In such instances, overlapping operations will not work, and we must turn to the next best compromise—linking operations in a pull system.

A pull system is a way of running a manufacturing process so that each operation, starting at the shipping dock and working back through the process, pulls the necessary product from the previous operation only as it is needed. This is in contrast to the traditional manufacturing cycle that makes product and then pushes it on to the next operation whether or not that operation is ready for it.

Toyota called this particular technique Kanban, and for a time Kanban was synonymous with JIT. Kanban is a Japanese word, one of the definitions of which is "card."

For a number of reasons, I would like to see the term Kanban disappear from discussions of Just In Time in an American context. First, the term has been used with several different meanings and continues to confuse. Second, I would prefer to see an American term used instead. Third, even in Japan there is not universal acceptance of the term Kanban. In fact, even within Toyota there are people who refer to this as the supermarket system, because, they tell us, the concept originated in the observation of American supermarkets by the Japanese.

The story is that a group of Toyota executives came to the United States in the 1950s to see how factories were run here. They came away from those visits with the conclusion that Americans tried to run factories much the same way the Japanese tried to run their factories. The Japanese designated this a push system.

A push system starts with an assembly schedule or a shipping schedule that is entered into the computer. The computer then "explodes" that schedule backward to the next level in the manufacturing process, adjusting it for lead time in order to tell the makers of subassemblies what subassemblies are needed and when. These subassembly requirements, also in the computer, are then exploded to the component level, and backed off for lead time, and on down through the entire manufacturing process to raw materials.

Paperwork goes out all along this process to tell people what to make and by when. Shop orders or schedules go to the factory. Purchase orders or releases go to suppliers.

Now begins the pushing. Each operation in that chain does its own thing and pushes it on to the next operation by a particular date. That operation knows it is coming, does its thing, and pushes it on by a certain date. The expectation is that all these things being pushed along will arrive at the same time on a particular date, so that assembly or shipping can happen on schedule.

Then, a week later the computer is run again to see how much of this really happened on schedule, what has changed, and what has to be rescheduled and replanned as a result of what did not happen on time. Then paperwork is sent out to trigger these changes and the process starts all over again. That, in simple form, is a push system.

While they were visiting the United States studying our ways of manufacturing, the Japanese also visited some supermarkets. They saw that the supermarket was run very differently from the factory, and from these observations of the supermarket in operation, the Japanese learned something that they took back to Japan and adapted to their factory operations.

In a supermarket, the customer determines what happens. Customers come to the supermarket, knowing that there are always going to be small quantities of whatever goods they need on the shelves. Because of this confidence that there will always be what is needed, they are content to take only small amounts and go away.

The customers know that when they come back, a day or a week later, the stocks will have been replenished and there will again be small amounts of everything they need on the shelves. They do not feel that it is necessary to hoard, to take a year's worth.

At frequent intervals a supermarket employee checks to see what the customers have taken. What has been taken is exactly what is put back on the shelf. In a supermarket there is no paperwork—no shop order or purchase order to tell the employee what items to put on the shelves. The customers, in effect, have told the employee what to put on the shelves by what they have taken off.

That is a pull system because the customer has determined what happens next. The customer in a very real sense pulls the rest of the operations, because he or she has put a specific demand on the business.

The Japanese took the concept and converted it into something that they could use to control factory operations. They created two kinds of signals—or Kanban. Assuming that the customer in this case is the assembly department, the first signal would constitute authorization—money, if you will—for the assembly department to go into its supermarket of needed material—subassemblies, components, raw material—and take a container of each item that is needed. These containers are very small and hold a measured quantity, usually an hour's worth or less. At Toyota, management must approve any container holding more than one-tenth of a day's supply.

In each container is the second type of Kanban—a production authorization. When and only when a container is removed from the "supermarket," this production authorization goes back to the supplying operation—whether that is another department or a supplier. It says: This signal is your authorization to produce another container full of parts. No more, no less. You have a given amount of time to do it.

An entire manufacturing process run using pull signals will look like the example in Figure 6.1. The process is like individual links in a chain. Assembly goes to its little supermarket and takes a container of what it needs, thereby releasing a production authorization signal to the preceding department—subassembly. This signal becomes the "money" for the subassembly department to go into its own little supermarket to pick up the components it needs. This releases authorizations to the preceding department as another link in the chain.

Theoretically, the only piece of paper—other than Kanban cards themselves—used in the entire process is the master assembly schedule for the assembly department. Given that the entire process runs on one piece of paper, that schedule must be very, very smooth.

Production control by Kanban

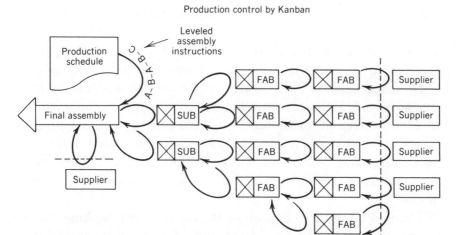

Figure 6.1. Production Control by Kanban

In this particular case, that master assembly schedule is to make an hour's worth of As, an hour's worth of Bs, a second hour's worth of As, a second hour's worth of Bs, and finally an hour's worth of Cs. That is a cycle, and that is the mix required for this period—40 percent As, 40 percent Bs, and 20 percent Cs. This is a very smooth schedule.

It should be clear that level loading is required to set the proper base for a successful Kanban system to work. Each customer tells each supplier what to do on an hourly basis. The process works like links in a chain. In order for this chain not to be broken, production must always be smooth and regular. If a customer came to a supplier and took a year's worth of something, the entire system would get thrown out of sync.

FLEXIBILITY

This system offers a great deal of flexibility. Suppose a customer, or the market in general, needs a different mix—more As and fewer Bs. (This can either be a change in the current market or a change in the forecast.)

To make such a change in a pull environment, the only paper that has to be changed is the master assembly schedule. When the final assembly is finished with its first hour's worth of As, the line goes back to the supermarket, not to pick up an hour's worth of what is needed for Bs but instead to pick up another hour's worth of what is needed for As. The line sends more A signals back down the chain to subassembly. Subassembly makes more As, sending more A signals for components back down the chain.

There is no need to find all of the shop orders, because there are none. There is no need to change all sorts of priorities, because they did not exist in the first place. Because this is a pull system, each feeder operation is waiting to find out what its customer needs hour by hour.

PERFECT JUST IN TIME HAS NO KANBAN SIGNALS

Many U.S. manufacturers have been too quick to establish a Kanban system and say "That is Just In Time." One reason for this is that the people most often responsible for introducing the concept of Just In Time to their companies have been the materials management or production and inventory control people. They see Kanban as a production control system—and even perhaps as the ultimate paperless shop-floor control system.

It is important to realize that a pefect Just-In-Time manufacturing environment has no Kanban signals in it. That is not to say that perfect JIT is not a pull system. In a perfect Just-In-Time environment, with one-at-a-time flow, each operation would still be pulling the previous operation, causing it to produce only at the rate needed. But there would be no need for signals if the flow were that perfect. A Kanban signal is a compromise, to be used only when perfect one-at-a-time flow cannot be reached.

PERFECT JIT

What would a perfect Just-In-Time environment look like?

Figure 6.1 shows fabricating operations linked together with pull signals. In an ideal world, those fabricating operations would all be performed in a work cell. A component would start at operation 1 and move from machine to machine one at a time until it was finished and ready for its customer, subassembly. In a work cell, there is no need for the machines to communicate with each other through Kanban signals. They are overlapped and the parts are flowing from one machine to another one at a time. In a perfect world, the work cell would be operating at exactly the rate required by the customer (cycle time), and would be able to change over as frequently as necessary to meet its customer needs (level loading). Then it could be fully integrated with its customer—in this case the subassembly department— feeding its customer components one at a time. Again, in a perfect world, this integrated line would be producing at exactly the rate and frequency required by its customer—final assembly. It could then feed directly into final assembly, creating a completely integrated manufacturing process where everything is moving one at a time.

In such a perfect world no Kanban signals are needed.

WHERE A KANBAN SYSTEM IS NEEDED

In the real world there will be many areas where it will be impossible to solve all problems and get to absolute one-at-a-time production. In such instances we are forced to continue to produce or move batches and a Kanban signal is a useful compromise, hopefully while ultimate solutions are found. Among the circumstances in which Kanban signals are necessary are:

1. When final assembly is done in one building and subas-

sembly is done in another building. It is physically impractical to move product one at a time over those distances.

2. When a feeding operation takes much longer to change over than a using department. It is not possible to get one-at-a-time flow with large discrepancies in changeover time. The feeding operation must run faster than the using department in order to get ahead and accumulate time for its long changeovers.

3. When a company would like to set up a number of different work cells but has only one machine available for an operation that must be done in each work cell. That machine must be put aside and linked to the work cells with Kanban signals so the various work cells can tell it what to do and when. This method makes it look as if the machine were an integral part of every work cell by sending frequent, small batches into each of the cells.

4. When a company does not dare put a troublesome machine into a work cell because of chronic maintenance problems that would bring the entire cell to a halt. Until the machine maintenance problem is solved, the machine must work alone at its own rate and be linked to other operations via Kanban signals.

5. When there are quality problems, bottlenecks, or capacity problems that don't allow operations to flow smoothly.

KANBAN CARDS

The Kanban signals themselves come in all sizes and shapes. The traditional signal is a card. On the card would be part number, type or size of container, number of pieces to be in that container, "supermarket" location, and how many cards of that nature there are in the system.

Companies that manufacture in an oily environment were the first to turn away from cards, which quickly become unreadable. So over the years a number of different signals have developed. Commonly used signals are metal plates affixed to baskets or tubs. These plates may display the same kind of information as on the cards or they may be simply color coded or uniquely shaped, or both.

Hewlett Packard simply puts yellow tape in a square on the floor. If the square is empty, that is the replenishment signal.

Cummins Engine uses numbered Ping-Pong balls.

General Motors sends computer-to-computer Kanban signals to its suppliers.

More and more frequently the containers themselves are the signals—both internally and with suppliers.

A KANBAN SYSTEM NEEDS SMALL LOT SIZES AND SHORT SETUP TIMES

When a system of Kanban signals is necessary, there are a number of keys to making that system work. The central key is for the supermarket to be replenished quickly and frequently. To do this, lot sizes must be reduced. To reduce lot sizes, it is necessary to reduce setup times.

Picture a supplying department that still has an 8-hour setup time on its machines and, because of the long setup time, still imposes a minimum requirement of a 16-hour run. Just as it begins to set up to run As, a Kanban signal is received from a using department requesting an hour's worth of B's. The next B's will not even start to be made for 32 working hours (24 hours to set up and run A's and 8 hours to set up for B's). If an hour from now the next signal asks for C's, it will not be honored for 55 working hours.

A supermarket that has to protect itself against 48-hour replenishment times is not a little supermarket, but a giant stockroom, which is what we are trying to eliminate in the first place.

JOB SHOPS

The pull system described here works in a simple repetitive environment, one with relatively few products. A pull system, however, will work equally as well in a complex repetitive situation, with thousands of different products, or even in a job shop, where each job will involve working with a completely different product.

But it has to be handled somewhat differently.

In a simple repetitive environment the signal is saying, "This is the authorization to replace exactly what has just been used." In a complex repetitive environment or a job shop, the signal would be the authorization to send whatever is next in line.

While the unit of measure in a simple repetitive environment is usually a part number and a quantity, in a complex situation or a job shop the item to be controlled may be expressed in terms of hours of work, or customer orders. The signal would be, "An hour's worth of work has just been taken; this is the authorization to put the next hour's worth of work into the supermarket," or "Another customer order has just been taken; this is the authorization to prepare the next order in the queue."

However the signal is expressed, the principle is the same—the using department is telling the supplying department what to do hour by hour.

VALUE-ADDED ANALYSIS

Figure 6.2 is an example of how a set of pull signals eliminated waste in the manufacturing process of an electronic cable assembly.

The pull signals were a compromise, but a compromise that was able to cut out half the steps in the manufacturing process—from 18 to nine steps. When true one-at-a-time manufacturing is instituted here, the process will be cut again by two-thirds—from nine steps to three.

Figure 6.2 shows seven loops, each of which represents operations that have been linked with a pull signal. In each of these seven loops, the company has accrued significant benefits in both inventory and lead-time reductions. In six of the seven

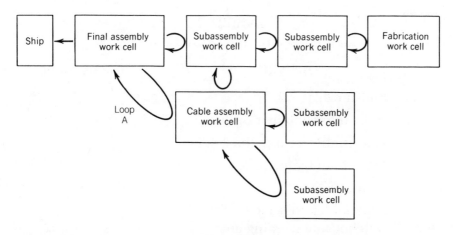

Figure 6.2.

loops, there were originally stockroom activities, requiring scheduling and release functions.

We have chosen loop A, between the cable subassembly and the final assembly, as representative of the change in any of the seven loops. Exhibits 6-1 and 6-2 show the value-added analysis of the process before implementing pull signals—18 activities, only two of which add value.

Exhibits 6-3 and 6-4 show that, by reducing lot sizes to a single container and linking operations with a pull signal, half of the activities disappear. Because final assembly schedules and controls cable assembly, scheduling department activities disappear. Because lot sizes are down to a single container, warehouse bulk storage and bulk material handling are eliminated. In addition, the final assembly incoming rack is now so small that it has been moved immediately adjacent to the assembly bench, eliminating another intermediate staging activity.

In addition to the elimination of nine non-value-adding activities and their related costs, this company saw drastic reductions in inventory and manufacturing throughput time. Under the old system, each of the seven loops in Figure 6.2 represented between one and three weeks inventory, as well as one to three

EXHIBIT 6-1
Linking Operations with a Pull Signal

	Activity	Adds Value
1.	Finish cable	X
2.	Place into container on bench	
3.	Wait (until batch is finished)	
4.	Move to outgoing rack	
5.	Wait	
6.	Material handler moves to warehouse, incoming area	
7.	Wait	
8.	Put into location	
9.	Wait	
	Scheduling department schedules release	
	Scheduling releases work order	
10.	Pull from location	
11.	Place on cart	
12.	Wait	
13.	Move to final assembly (incoming rack)	
14.	Wait	
15.	Move next to assembly bench	
16.	Wait	
17.	Move to workplace	
18.	Assemble	X

EXHIBIT 6-2
Summary of Value-Added Analysis

Type of Activity	Number	Percent of Total
Value added	2	11
Wait	7	38
Move	5	28
Other	4	22

EXHIBIT 6-3
Value Added (After Linking Operations)

Activity	Adds Value
1. Finish cable	X
2. Place into container on bench	
3. Wait (until container is full)	
4. Move container to Point of Pickup (POP) stand	
5. Wait	
6–12 (Out)	
13. Move to incoming POP stand	
14. Wait	
15–16 (Out)	
17. Move to workplace	
18. Assemble	

EXHIBIT 6-4
Value-Added Summary

Type of Activity	Before	After	Improvement
Value added	2	2	—
Wait	7	3	57%
Move	5	3	40%
Other	4	1	75%
Total	18	9	50%

weeks of throughput time. Today, these loops each represent approximately one hour's worth of inventory and one hour of throughput time. This company boasts of turning its work-in-process inventory in excess of 120 times per year.

As extraordinary as these results seem, this company recognizes that it has not reached perfect one-at-a-time manufacturing, that its pull system is a compromise. When the company reaches the ultimate of one-at-a-time flow, it will eliminate six of the nine current steps in each of its loops. Cable assembly will be integrated with final assembly and the steps will be:

1. Finish cable.
2. Place onto final assembly workplace.
3. Assemble.

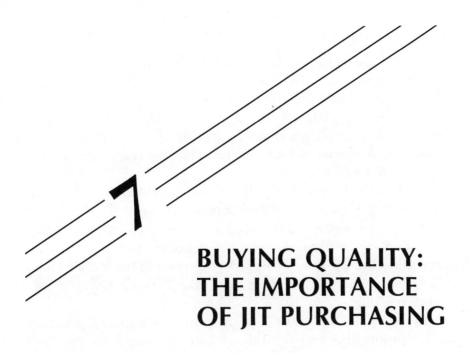

BUYING QUALITY:
THE IMPORTANCE
OF JIT PURCHASING

The typical cost breakdown for a U.S. manufacturer is 70 percent purchased material and components, 10 percent direct labor, and 20 percent overhead. This means that the typical purchasing department spends more than twice as much money as all other functions in the organization put together. It also means that a five percent reduction in purchase prices would have the same impact on bottom-line profit as the elimination of 35 percent of all direct labor.

But cost is not the only major impact suppliers have on companies. Their quality can make or break a product. In addition, response time to customers is often dictated more by lead times from suppliers than by a company's internal lead times.

A company cannot become a world-class manufacturer until it

has developed a true partnership with its suppliers and successfully made strides with them in quality, lead time, and cost. Just-In-Time purchasing offers the framework for that partnership.

Just-In-Time purchasing is as different from traditional purchasing as Just-In-Time manufacturing is from traditional manufacturing. And what it wants to accomplish is exactly the same—the elimination of waste.

There are three different categories of waste that need to be addressed for a company to implement successful JIT.

First is the waste in a company's own manufacturing process: the counting, storing, moving, inspection, scheduling, rework, and other things we have been dealing with in the last six chapters. These wastes, as we have seen, take 99 percent of all manufacturing time.

A second set of wastes is in the purchasing process itself, in the relationships and control mechanisms between buyer and seller.

A third set of wastes is in the manufacturing process of a company's suppliers. They would tend to be the same kinds of wastes found in a company's own manufacturing process.

Because the average manufacturing company in the United States finds that 70 percent of its costs are purchased material and components, eventually every company must get into that third category of wastes and help its suppliers eliminate waste in their manufacturing process.

But before a company can help its suppliers eliminate waste in their process, it must first eliminate waste in its own manufacturing process, then work to eliminate wastes in the purchasing process itself.

ELIMINATING WASTES IN THE PURCHASING PROCESS

Once a company has a source of supply and a negotiated price, there are a number of other things that go on in the purchasing process that do not add value to the product. A purchase order does not add value to the product. An amendment to the purchase order does not add value. Acknowledgments, receiving reports, and invoices do not add value. Taking something off a truck and putting it onto a central receiving dock does not add value. Moving it to a holding area does not add value. Inspecting it does not add value. Putting it in the stockroom does not add value. Counting it does not add value. Taking it from a large container and putting it into a small container does not add value. Moving it to the point where it is going to be used does not add value. Transportation cost does not add value.

None of these things add value, and yet they are typically part of what is done in managing the control mechanisms between buyer and seller. The purpose of Just-In-Time purchasing is to eliminate those wastes.

The big question is: How does a company go about it?

There is only one place to start. That is with quality.

It is necessary to eliminate the need for incoming inspection. Recently, in one of my seminars, someone said to me, "JIT purchasing increases my risk because its objective is to eliminate incoming inspection." My response was, "We have to change a few of your words around. JIT purchasing *decreases* your risk because its objective is not to rely on incoming inspection for quality. It is necessary for a company to insure quality long before incoming inspection."

But incoming inspection cannot be eliminated by writing a memo that says: As of tomorrow there will be no inspection. Making inspection unnecessary is a lot of hard work. It takes problem solving. It takes people working with the supplier's people, making sure they understand the process and solve the problems in the process. The minimum result of this is that the company is satisfied with the supplier's inspection procedures so they don't have to be duplicated.

Far better is that the suppliers understand their own process and control their process well enough that they are doing it right the first time, so that monitoring can take the place of inspection.

CHANGING RELATIONSHIPS

Unfortunately, it is impossible to put in that kind of hard work and effort with the kinds of traditional relationships companies have had in purchasing. So the start of Just-In-Time purchasing is to develop a new set of relationships.

The traditional relationship between buyer and seller has been adversarial. Companies want three quotes, and they had better pick the lowest one or have a very good reason for not doing so. They want to make sure suppliers keep their pencils sharp, because six months from now the company is going out again for quotes, and if the current supplier is not the low bidder he may not get the next six months of business.

And companies would like to know suppliers' costs, because it is obvious they are making obscene profits. Companies would like to negotiate away some of those obscene profits into cost reductions or cost avoidances.

But that's a two-way street. Suppliers are thinking in the same terms—they may not get the next six months' worth of business. How much risk and investment are they willing to put into this? Not very much. Suppliers want to make sure they are profitable now because they might not be here six months from now.

In 1957 Ernest Anderson developed the concept of systems contracting. Systems contracting was and is not very far away from what we now call Just-In-Time purchasing. Anderson has been out there for over 20 years helping people implement systems contracting. But he has not had nearly as much press about it as he might because the companies that implement this tend to implement it on nonproductive items—things that would typically come from warehouse distributors such as maintenance supplies, plumbing supplies, electrical supplies, and pens and pencils.

Some companies have implemented systems contracting for raw materials and purchased components with fantastic success, but not enough so that a great deal has been heard about it.

Systems contracting was the first recognition that instead of an adversarial relationship, there can be common benefits for buyer and seller in the purchasing process. Under Just-In-Time purchasing, we want to carry that relationship a step further.

The new relationship we want is a long-term, mutually beneficial relationship with fewer but better suppliers. This relationship consists of four elements:

Long term

Mutual benefit

Fewer suppliers

Better suppliers

This idea goes right back to eliminating waste. In order to eliminate the waste of incoming inspection a company must put in the hard work, resources, and time to solve problems, and develop a track record of mutual trust with suppliers. This simply cannot be done with thousands of suppliers. It cannot be done if suppliers change every six months when a company goes out for bids again. It can only be done if a company has one or two suppliers for each commodity. Relationships must be developed that are long term, mutually beneficial, with fewer but better suppliers.

Long term, because it takes a long time to solve the problems

Mutually beneficial, because this is the only way to make them long term

Fewer suppliers, because no company has the resources to do this with many suppliers

Better suppliers, because the entire process hinges on quality

XEROX: A PERFECT EXAMPLE

Once a company has started solving the problems of incoming inspection, the sky is the limit on eliminating other wastes. Special arrangements can be developed to eliminate paperwork. Freight costs, handling, and inventories can be reduced.

Let me use Xerox as an example of one of the leaders in implementing Just-In-Time purchasing. In 1985 *Purchasing Magazine* awarded Xerox the annual Medal of Professional Excellence. This was a recognition of five years of hard work by Xerox to streamline its purchasing process and change relationships with its suppliers.

In 1980, Xerox centralized its purchasing operation and found that it had 5000 suppliers. By 1985, Xerox had cut the number to 300; by early 1987 the number was on its way to 260 and the word is that Xerox believes 150 is an even better number.

Xerox began to work with suppliers on quality in the suppliers' processes in 1980 or 1981. By 1985, approximately 75 percent of Xerox's suppliers had been certified, meaning that incoming inspection was no longer necessary. That 75 percent of the suppliers accounted for more than 90 percent of the product Xerox purchased.

Xerox has also kept meticulous records of the problems in assembly from parts that still go through incoming inspection compared with those that do not. The company finds twice as many problems with those parts that still require incoming inspection. These are not problems that appear at inspection. These are problems that appear after the parts successfully pass incoming inspection. Xerox is not taking additional risks—the quality is far better on parts that are certified than on those that are still going through the traditional incoming inspection.

In 1985, Xerox took further advantage of its progress in quality and in reducing the number of suppliers by starting an experiment called the bus route. It chose 25 suppliers that (1) were certified—incoming inspection no longer required—and (2) were within a 40-mile radius of Rochester, New York, where Xerox is located.

There is nothing magic about 40 miles. It was just a convenient, logical place to start. The experiment was such a success that in late 1986 Xerox began to develop a similar bus route for suppliers in Chicago, hundreds of miles away.

In the initial experiment the Xerox bus (actually a truck) goes to each of the 25 suppliers each day and picks up a day's worth of every item those suppliers provide—about 110 different products or parts. The truck picks up the same quantity of every item every day for a fixed production period.

This took a lot of effort on Xerox's part. At the same time Xerox was paring its supplier list from 5000 to 300 and certifying about 225 of those companies, it was also smoothing its own assembly operation so that by 1985 Xerox had a smooth, repeatable demand for purchased components.

The quantities picked up each day are small—40 of this and 60 of that. This is not to say that each supplier is producing each item every day; some are but many are not.

Xerox, however, cannot be accused of simply pushing back inventory on to suppliers. It is actively working with suppliers to get them to produce a day's worth every day. Xerox wants its relationships with these suppliers to be long term and mutually beneficial.

Xerox picks up in an afternoon what will be used the next production day and shipped the day after in the form of finished goods.

Think of how simple life can be with these 110 items. The truck arrives every day and goes immediately to the area where the parts are used. Now there is no need for a central receiving dock or a holding area. There is no need for incoming inspection anymore; Xerox and its suppliers have spent a long time making that unnecessary. There is no need for a stockroom or a locator system. There is no need for picking and transporting.

The next step for Xerox was to realize that packaging does not add value. The original practice was to receive product in corrugated boxes, which were cut or ripped open and thrown away. Xerox developed returnable, recyclable plastic containers—containers that are appropriate for use by the suppliers to pack product in at the end of their manufacturing process; appropriate to be trucked, whether 40 miles or from Chicago; and appropriate to be used at the assembly line in the plant without changing containers. Ultimately, these containers will be used to eliminate purchase orders by being the Kanban signal that goes back to the supplier and says: This is your authorization to produce more.

The next logical area for Xerox to tackle is the waste of receiving reports. In 1987, the company was carefully thinking through the purpose of receiving reports. It was in no way positive that eliminating receiving reports would be feasible; it was merely challenging the common wisdom of receiving reports.

The first purpose is to know something has been received. But that is unnecessary in a bus system—Xerox knows every morning if something has not arrived. Not being able to produce because something has not arrived is a much more drastic way of knowing than is making out 110 pieces of paper every day. Also, after a while the truck driver knows what is supposed to be loaded on his truck each day at each stop, and can call his supervisor if there are deviations.

The second purpose of a receiving report is to start the process of payment. It goes into a file in accounts payable so when the invoice arrives, the receiving report can be taken back out of the file and matched with the invoice and payment can be processed.

But all of this activity (including the invoice) does not add value. Xerox is thinking that because material is received in the afternoon, used the next day, and shipped the day after as finished goods, the company's own computer can be used to immediately begin processing payment on the 110 parts for those 25 suppliers. The payment would be keyed to shipment—if Xerox shipped a product, the parts must have been in it.

Xerox is still only thinking about this step. The company is looking to see if there are legal and tax questions that must be answered before this step can be taken.

The point to keep in mind, however, is that Xerox could not even be thinking about this if it were still dealing with 5000 suppliers. It could not be thinking about this if it were still receiving a month's worth of product every month, inspecting it, rejecting some and keeping some, putting it in stockrooms, and taking out a day's worth every day. And when the supply is down to about two weeks, another month's worth comes in and the process starts all over again.

The net result of all this activity has been to reduce the price of purchased product by 40 to 50 percent across the board. At the same time, Xerox has reduced the cost of the purchasing and material control functions by over 60 percent.

Xerox has carried its thinking so far that it is actually frightening people.

The logic process goes something like this: In 1980 there were 5000 suppliers submitting invoices. By early 1987 there were only 260. Someday soon there may be as few as 150. For 25 of the current suppliers, a way has been developed to eliminate invoices. Is there even a need for an accounts payable department anymore?

Of course, Xerox may not ever be able to do away with its accounts payable department altogether. But it is questioning the way business is conducted in ways that were unthinkable without JIT purchasing. It is raising questions and making changes in ways that would be unthinkable without long-term, mutually beneficial relationships with fewer but better suppliers.

SINGLE SOURCING

The relationship of fewer but better, when carried to its logical extreme, will move U.S. manufacturers more and more to single sources.

The concept of single sourcing is as troublesome to traditional purchasing people as slower run speeds and smaller lots are to traditional manufacturing people.

The two most common objections to single sourcing are:

What if there is a strike?

How does a company know it is getting the best price possible if it only has one supplier?

I would hope that anyone who asks the first question is talking about a wildcat strike. Because if a purchasing agent has only one supplier for a commodity, is not aware that it is contract negotiation time, and fails to protect against the possibility of a strike, that person should not be in purchasing. Therefore we must be talking about a wildcat strike, and those just do not happen very often anymore in this country. In the U.S. this objection is a cop-out.

Outside this country, it is harder to be sure that a wildcat strike will not take place and, depending on the particular country, this may preclude single sourcing; but it shouldn't preclude a minimum number of suppliers.

As to the issue of price, if a company approaches JIT purchasing the right way, price will not be a problem. While a company is reducing the number of suppliers, it is getting the best price due to traditional competition. Also, if the correct process is used for selecting a single source, the result should always be the best price. There are five most important criteria when choosing suppliers:

Quality

Willingness to work together

Technical competence

Geography

Price

Although price is listed as the fifth criteria, it is, in many ways, a given. The correct process is to select the best supplier based on the first four criteria and then make sure the supplier meets the fifth criterion of best price. In most cases the best supplier will already offer the best price. In all other cases, if the best supplier has been chosen, it will be possible to work with that supplier to identify what problems must be solved to get quickly to the best price.

At this point, the JIT purchasing relationship comes into play to make sure the supplier always has the best price. This is one of the most significant departures from traditional purchasing. Rather than the traditional purchasing model, where the purchaser sits back and defends against the inevitable attempt to raise price, in a JIT relationship the purchaser and supplier actively work together to continually lower the cost of purchased material. This must be done without reducing the supplier's profit margin.

This is done in a number of ways.

The purchaser can take advantage of the supplier's technical knowledge of his or her own process to reexamine tolerances and other specifications in order to make the product easier or cheaper to manufacture.

The purchaser can help the supplier implement Just-In-Time manufacturing in order to eliminate waste in his or her own process.

The purchaser and supplier can work together and get early involvement of the supplier in designing new products—again using the supplier's knowledge—to design products using new or cheaper materials and processes.

The kinds of continuous, problem-solving, cost- and price-reducing relationships necessary to make these constant improvements cannot be developed with thousands of suppliers. Nor can they be developed with suppliers that are changing every six months based on new quotes. They can be developed with one or two suppliers for each commodity a company purchases.

Needed are long-term, mutually beneficial relationships with fewer but better suppliers.

TIMING

JIT purchasing should be brought into the total JIT implementation process at a specific time.

Quality comes first. The move from quality at incoming inspection to quality at the supplier's production facility—certification—should be started immediately. The reduction in the number of suppliers can also start immediately.

But trying to achieve JIT delivery from suppliers should come last, only after a company has made major gains implementing JIT within its own four walls. The key thing a company must accomplish before it gets JIT delivery is a smooth, predictable, reliable requirement.

Beyond quality and the relationship with suppliers, the key to Xerox starting the bus route was being able to say to suppliers: We will take the same amount from you every day for the next 20 days. To get to that point a company has to implement just about all of Just In Time. A company must:

Solve internal quality problems and equipment breakdown problems

Initiate level loading and cycle time

Initiate a pull system (with or without signals)

If the purchaser is unpredictable, the supplier cannot possibly produce the product as required and must defend against the purchaser's unpredictability with inventory. This can lead to a feeling that the purchaser is pushing inventory back onto the supplier, and can hinder the long-term, mutually beneficial relationship.

VALUE-ADDED ANALYSIS

The following value-added analysis of the Xerox purchasing process will show the steps taken out of the process, first by the quality program which eliminated incoming inspection and, second, by the bus route that allowed Xerox to pick up a day's worth of 110 items each day and deliver them exactly where needed in the shop.

EXHIBIT 7-1
Value-Added Analysis
Xerox Purchased Component

Activity	Adds Value	Distance Traveled (feet)
1. Move into dock		
2. Wait on truck (for package count verification)		
3. Move from truck to flow lane (onto slave pallet)		25
4. Flow (automatically) to last pallet in line		15
5. Wait, move, wait (one pallet length at a time)		20
6. Move to receiving clerk		5
7. Wait Input to system Inspection instructions Receiving paperwork		
8. Move to split station		25
9. Remove carton from pallet		
10. Open carton		
11. Remove sample quantity from carton		
12. Repack sample quantity		
13. Put onto inspection pallet		
14. Wait (2–3 hours or until pallet is full)		
15. Move (automatically) to outgoing area conveyor (main lot routed to holding area)		65
16. Wait (for trucker)		

EXHIBIT 7-1 (continued)

Activity	Adds Value	Distance Traveled (feet)
17. Move with fork truck into truck at receiving dock		25
18. Wait		
19. Drive to Building 208		3000
20. Move from truck to location rack		150
21. Wait (until priority list calls for inspection)		
22. Move carton to inspector's bench		50
23. Inspect		

24. Wait
    Input to system
    Release of original lot		

25. Move back to location rack		50
26. Wait (until parts required)		
27. Move into truck		150
28. Wait		
29. Drive to receiving dock		3000
30. Move to flow lane (onto slave pallet)		25
31. Move (automatically) to outgoing area conveyor		55
32. Wait (for automated train to arrive)		
33. Move from conveyor to floor		10
34. Stack two high		
35. Move from floor to automated train		20
36. Wait (for train to be filled and programmed)		
37. Move (automatically) to assembly station		600

38.	Wait (for fork truck)	
39.	Offload into buffer area	25
40.	Wait	
41.	Move to detrashing incoming conveyor	120
42.	Wait	
43.	Convey to operator station	40
44.	Raise into work station	5
45.	Detrash and determine location	
46.	Move onto correct cart	10
47.	Wait (until cart full)	
48.	Push cart to outer edge of area	10
49.	Wait (for dispatcher)	
50.	Move cart to flow lane access aisle	100
51.	Move carton into correct flow lane location	5
52.	Wait (until operator needs)	
53.	Assemble	X

Total Distance Traveled: 7610 feet (nearly 1.5 miles)

EXHIBIT 7-2
Value-Added Summary

Activity	Number	% of Total
Value added	1	2
Wait	18	34
Move	23	43
Other	11	21
Total	53	100

EXHIBIT 7-3
Value-Added Analysis
After Eliminating Incoming Inspection
(Certification)

Activity	Adds Value	Distance Traveled (feet)
1. Move into dock		
2. Wait on truck (for package count verification)		
3. Move from truck to flow lane (onto slave pallet)		25
4. Flow (automatically) to last pallet in line		15
5. Wait, move, wait (one pallet length at a time)		20
6. Move to receiving clerk		5
7. Wait Input to system Receiving paperwork		
8–30 (Out)		
31. Move (automatically) to outgoing area conveyor		55
32. Wait (for automated train to arrive)		
33. Move from conveyor to floor		10
34. Stack two high		
35. Move from floor onto automated train		20
36. Wait (for train to be filled and programmed)		
37. Move (automatically) to assembly station		600
38. Wait (for fork truck)		

39.	Offload into buffer area	25
40.	Wait	
41.	Move to detrashing incoming conveyor	120
42.	Wait	
43.	Convey to operator station	40
44.	Raise into work station	5
45.	Detrash and determine location	
46.	Move onto correct cart	10
47.	Wait (until cart is full)	
48.	Push cart to outer edge of area	10
49.	Wait (for dispatcher)	
50.	Move cart to flow lane access aisle	100
51.	Move carton onto correct flow lane location	5
52.	Wait (until operator needs)	
53.	Assemble	X

Total distance traveled: 1065 feet

EXHIBIT 7-4
Value-Added Summary
After Eliminating Inspection
(Certification)

Activity	Number Before	Number After
Value added	1	1
Wait	18	11
Move	23	13
Other	11	5
Total	53	30

EXHIBIT 7-5
Value-Added Analysis
After Bus Route

Activity		Adds Value	Distance Traveled (feet)
1.	Move into dock		
2.	Wait on truck (for pickup confirmation)		
3–7	(Out)		
8–30	(Out, quality)		
31–49	(Out)		
50.	Move (cart) to flow lane access aisle*		100
51.	Move carton into correct flow lane location		5
52.	Wait (until operator needs)		
53.	Assemble	X	

Total Distance Traveled 105 feet

*Color-coded containers are picked up from each supplier's dock and put into color-coded carts already on the truck, so the material handler at Xerox can roll carts out of the truck directly down the corresponding color-coded aisles to where they are needed.

134

EXHIBIT 7-6
Value-Added Summary
After Eliminating Inspection and Bus Route

Activity	Number Beginning	Number After Quality	Number After Bus Route
Value added	1	1	1
Wait	18	11	2
Move	23	13	3
Other	11	5	0
TOTAL	53	30	6

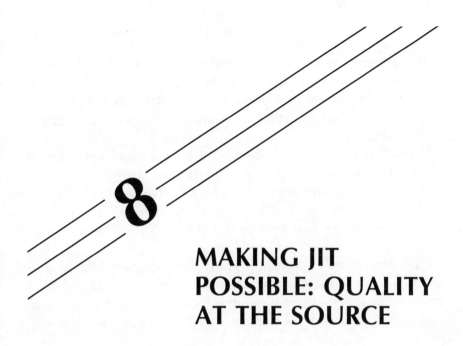

8

MAKING JIT
POSSIBLE: QUALITY
AT THE SOURCE

The story of Hutchinson Technology in the book's introduction contains an important lesson about quality. Hutchinson's president determined that JIT could not be successful until the company had drastically improved its quality.

The lesson is simple, yet profound. JIT can only be successful in a company that is producing quality goods. JIT and quality are inextricably linked. Quality makes JIT possible.

Remember the definition and purpose of JIT—production of the smallest possible quantity at the latest possible time using a minimum of resources, and elimination of waste in the manufacturing process.

If a company is ever going to reach perfect one-at-a-time man-ufacturing, there is no time to redo parts. If a good part is not made the first time, and every time, production will be shut down. Without quality production, there is no way to eliminate inventories.

As stated in Chapter 1, there is a two-pronged approach to eliminating waste; one is flow, the other is quality.

The kind of quality necessary in a JIT environment is quality at the source, with an emphasis on doing it right the first time. Doing it right the first time is not the traditional approach to quality.

The traditional approach—known as after-the-fact assess-ment—is to produce a product, then inspect it, sort the good from the bad, hope there is enough good to satisfy the customer, and hope the bad can be salvaged. In this traditional approach, the source of quality is seen as the inspection bench.

The kind of quality needed by JIT—quality at the source, or before-the-fact prevention—focuses on quality at the operator, the machine, and the process; quality at the supplier's operator, the supplier's machine, or the supplier's process.

There is a three-step approach to get from after-the-fact assess-ment to before-the-fact prevention. The first is defining require-ments. Second is getting the process under control. And third is maintaining control of the process once it is under control.

STEP 1: DEFINING REQUIREMENTS

I think the major contribution made by Phil Crosby, one of the gurus of quality, is his conception of how Western manufactur-ers have gone wrong in their thinking of quality. Crosby feels Westerners define quality wrong—as perfection, as roundness or beauty, or as something that cannot really be measured or ever truly reached. Crosby argues that the true definition of quality is meeting requirements.

Every company says it has good clear specifications. But most do not. Whenever somebody says, "That is good enough," a red flag should go up. That is not a clear specification.

Clear specifications do not mean that everything has to reach the same specifications. This is a difficult concept. It means that if a Ford Pinto meets its customers' requirements as well as a Cadillac meets its customers' requirements, then the Pinto is just as much a quality car as a Cadillac.

Once people have accepted the definition of quality as meeting requirements rather than perfection, the whole concept of zero defects changes. The question is no longer: Can this product always be produced perfectly? Rather, the question becomes: Can this product always be produced so it meets requirements? This takes quality out of the realm of near impossibility and brings it well within reach.

There are two kinds of customers and each has its own set of requirements. The ultimate consumers, who pay for the goods and services, are the external customers. But equally important are the host of internal customers within the process.

Total quality is more than the quality of the product shipped to a customer. Total quality is the end result of a whole string of activities. In order to ensure that the product is shipped right every time, there must be total quality relationships between employees and customers as well as employees and suppliers, and, equally important, between employees and employees.

Quality must be the ultimate goal of the salesperson, the customer service representative, the design engineer, the marketing manager, and the human resources manager.

A major part of getting into a quality program is to begin to work more closely from one department to another. Frequently, departments don't talk to each other enough, and they don't trust each other. Sometimes, engineers tighten tolerances and specifications because they do not believe the manufacturing department will do its best to meet the specifications. Manufacturing, on the other hand, remembers the times in the past when it has not met specifications and things have turned out fine. The natural tendency in this case is to take further liberties and not meet current specifications.

This conflict between engineering and manufacturing is common in the West. There is almost a palpable wall between the two departments. This leads to the perception that engineers design a product and throw it over the wall to be manufactured. Manufacturing is angry because of design specifications that are unreasonable, and engineering is equally angry at the manufacturing "dummies" who cannot manufacture items to their specifications.

The Japanese have solved that problem by turning it around—putting the burden of proof, so to speak, on engineering. The Japanese assume that when something is difficult to manufacture, it must have been designed wrong. Another Japanese practice is for the development people to go out on the shop floor for the first 90 days of the introduction of a new product. They stay with it until such time as the manufacturing process is acceptable, the key characteristics have been identified, and process control charts on the key characteristics have been set up and are under control. The point is that manufacturing and engineering are each other's customers and must know each other's true requirements before they can design or manufacture right the first time.

STEP 2: GETTING THE PROCESS UNDER CONTROL

The second step of the three-step road to prevention is to get the process under control. There are two pieces to getting the process under control. The first is operator involvement, because the operator is a key to quality. The second piece is problem solving. Problem solving begins with data gathering, in order to find out just how big the problem is. Operator involvement begins with getting the operator to be his or her own inspector and to participate in data gathering to identify problems. It is a fact of life that there are problems in every process, so there will virtually always be a need for problem solving.

There is a right way and a wrong way to problem solve.

The right way is to use whatever diagnostic tools are necessary to find the root cause or causes of the problem, so that the final step in solving any problem is to ask, What can be done so this problem never has to be solved again? The proof that the root cause has been found is that the problem can be turned off and turned back on again. It is not human nature to turn a problem back on, but unless a company can do it, the company will never know if the real root cause has been found.

The far more common, and wrong, way to solve a problem is with the shotgun approach, doing everything possible to try to get the problem to go away. Even if the problem does go away, no one knows what made it go away. The company is content to be producing again.

There are a number of diagnostic tools and techniques for finding root causes. My colleagues and I sat down in 1986 and came up with almost 100 techniques formal enough to have a name.

These techniques range from the very simple, such as ABC analysis and matrix analysis, to the very complex, such as designed experiments.

In most industries, our experience is that those tools that are readily usable by people on the shop floor will be appropriate for roughly 85 percent of the problems. It is only for the last 15 percent of the problems that statisticians, quality engineers, and other specialists are needed.

STEP 3: KEEPING THE PROCESS UNDER CONTROL

There are three parts to keeping the process under control once control has been achieved.

The first is an even greater degree of operator involvement than was necessary during the time when control was being achieved. Second is statistical process control (SPC), including precontrol. The third is fail-safing.

In the second step—getting the process under control—the operator was involved in self-inspection and in gathering data about the process. In the third step—keeping the process under control—the role of the operator must be expanded from one of involvement to one of control.

Operator control requires three elements. The first is good clear specifications (defining requirements). The second is feedback mechanisms such as process control charts. The third is the ability to take corrective action—with both tools and training.

SPC is primarily a feedback mechanism for the operator to use to control the process. SPC sets up control limits for the process to perform within, and monitors—usually on a sample basis—how the process is performing, calling for corrective action when defects appear.

A further refinement of SPC is precontrol, which means that the corrective action is taken before defects appear rather than after.

The most appropriate use of statistical process control is to keep a process under control. Too many companies bypass the step of defining requirements, bypass the step of getting the process under control through problem solving, and immediately jump into statistical process control. They end up trying to keep something under control that was never under control to begin with.

SPC is also most appropriate when dealing with dimensional problems—problems that are easily measured such as length, size, or tolerance. Most companies find a significant number of quality problems that are not dimensional in nature, but have to do more with workmanship or one-time problems, such as misidentified parts, missed operations, burrs, contamination, or setting up equipment incorrectly.

Fail-safing, the third method to keep the process under control, is more appropriate to deal with this kind of quality problem.

Fail-safing is figuring out how to make it easy to do something correctly and difficult or impossible to do it incorrectly. Social scientists have long shown experimentally that, given a correct procedure and an incorrect procedure, people will invariably choose the correct procedure *if it is as easy to perform as the incorrect procedure.* Fail-safing can be applied at the inspection, in the process itself, or in the product design.

A fail-safed inspection would detect a defect and signals would go on—lights, buzzers—and people would know that a defective piece had been made.

A fail-safed process is one that checks itself before it begins an operation or during the process, to prevent a defect in the first place. There are self-checking fixtures that will not turn on if not set up properly. One consumer products company put touch-sensitive monitors under each pile of the four different documents that had to be packaged with each item, so that if the operator did not pick up a document from each pile the box would not cycle on to the next operation.

Fail-safing a product design is designing a product for "manu-facturability." All products are designed with the customer in mind. Fail-safing takes the operators and manufacturing process into account as well, and makes the product easy to manufacture correctly.

A number of years ago an auto company had to call back cars because a baffle in the gas tank had been installed backwards on a number of cars. The company took this opportunity to fail-safe the gas tank through a redesign. It redesigned the mounting tabs to be nonsymmetrical, so the baffle simply could not fit if it were installed backwards.

For many companies, fail-safing becomes an almost equal partner to SPC.

THE RELATIONSHIP BETWEEN JIT AND QUALITY

While quality does not need JIT to be successful, a JIT environment does enhance any quality effort in terms of both philosophy and practice. The things JIT will do to establish balance and flow, eliminate waste, and foster the principle of continuous improvement will all help enable a company to reach a total quality environment more rapidly.

The traditional motto of total quality has been: Do It Right The First Time. There is now a growing awareness that that is not enough, and people are modifying this statement to: Do The Right Things Right The First Time. But people are still not completely sure what the right things are.

This is where JIT can make a significant contribution to total quality—by defining the right things as those things that add value. For instance, a process we recently analyzed determined that 18 to 20 percent of the activities and cost involved in a particular process was due to not doing it right the first time. The total quality opportunity was 18 to 20 percent.

Analyzing the same process from a JIT point of view showed that fully 80 percent of the activities did not add value. JIT would work to eliminate as much of that 80 percent as possible, and total quality would then focus on doing the remaining 20 percent right the first time.

DAY TO DAY

In regard to day-to-day implementation on the shop floor, JIT needs from quality a predictable process. Ultimately, for perfect JIT, a company needs perfect quality. But for initial implementation, JIT needs a predictable rather than perfect process.

Figure 8.1 demonstrates what is meant by predictable. Both Product A and Product B have patterns of defects that add up over time to about five percent loss.

Product B is by no means perfect, although it is predictable, always losing between 4 ½ and six percent, while Product A is not predictable, averaging five percent loss but having periods of much higher loss.

It is possible to implement JIT around Product B because of its predictability. Trying to implement JIT around Product A would

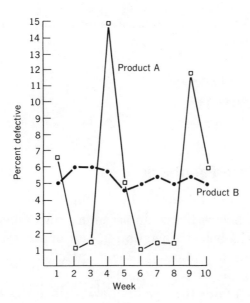

Figure 8.1.

actually amplify the pain and problems associated with periods of high loss. In the case of Product A, quality problems must be worked out first, and JIT should be held off until a level of predictability is reached.

This example uses yield to demonstrate the point, but predictability is needed not only in terms of yield, but in equipment uptime and the process itself.

Companies that have quality problems needing to be solved before implementing JIT need to be careful not to let the pendulum swing so far that they insist on perfect quality before implementing JIT. Remember, the process needs only to be predictable. And the entire process does not need to be predictable before JIT can be implemented in a portion of the process.

WHAT JIT BRINGS TO QUALITY

Specifically, JIT brings a number of unique elements to a total quality/Just-In-Time environment. These elements reduce defect rates and cost of quality, and create a better environment for permanently solving problems. These JIT contributions are:

Immediate feedback

Slower run speeds

Stopping the process

Immediate Feedback

To understand immediate feedback, think about Henry Ford's assembly line before it was an assembly line. Operation 1 was done two weeks before operation 2, and operation 2 was done the day before operation 3. Each operation is producing a month's worth of parts at a time.

If operation 3 finds that the first few parts it tries to work with are bad, and that the problem occurred during operation 1, it has two problems.

One problem is that it has a month's worth of parts to inspect, then redo or scrap.

The other problem is that the trail is cold. The defect happened two weeks ago, and operation 1 has changed over and is now making another product. It is extremely difficult to find out exactly what went wrong, to get to the root cause.

But after implementation of JIT, this type of quality problem is not caught in two weeks, or in a day, but in a matter of minutes later. Now, instead of two month's worth of defects, there are only minutes worth of defects. Also, finding problems a couple of minutes after they begin (and while they are still happening) rather than a couple of weeks later helps a company find root causes of those problems, making possible permanent solutions so the problems never have to be solved again.

Also, in a JIT environment, since each successive operation potentially constitutes a 100 percent inspection of previous operations, it can eliminate separate inspection operations after those previous operations. This not only eliminates the cost of non-value-adding activities, but is a more thorough quality check.

Slower Run Speeds

As has been shown, a major building block of JIT is to operate equipment at the rate the product is required rather than as fast as possible. Slowing equipment down almost always has a beneficial effect on the predictability of the process.

These benefits accrue both when the feeds and speeds are adjusted, or when the machinery waits a measured amount of time between cycles and the feeds and speeds are left alone.

Those benefits take the form of:

Lower defect rates

Less variability (production within narrower control limits)

Longer tool life

Less equipment breakdown

These contribute to the predictability of the process that is so vital to the continued success of JIT.

Stopping The Process

Another major building block of JIT is stopping the process when problems occur. As has been said before, stopping the process is not the worst thing in the world—as has been thought in traditional manufacturing. Rather, it is only the third-worst thing in the world, ranking behind making another defective part and letting another problem happen without finding a permanent solution.

Stopping the process should be used to create the necessary pain to make sure the right kind of attention is being paid to the problem, so the first or second worst things don't happen any more.

JIT FORCES NEW MAINTENANCE PRACTICES

A key part of process predictability is equipment reliability. Companies getting involved in JIT see that current maintenance practices do not foster this. Many companies have been looking to preventive maintenance to solve their problems of machine reliability.

But preventive maintenance is only a portion of what is needed—total productive maintenance (TPM). Companies that think they can solve all machine reliability issues with preventive maintenance are like companies that think they can solve all product reliability problems with SPC. Preventive maintenance is to total productive maintenance what SPC is to total quality.

JIT forces a company to go into total productive maintenance to develop an environment of predictability from the point of view of the equipment. Total productive maintenance is a term that was coined by General Electric back in the early 1950s, but has been sadly neglected in this country since then. It has been picked up by some of the leading edge Japanese companies.

The philosophy parallels that of total quality. While total quality moves from an emphasis on inspection, sorting, and rework to an emphasis on prevention, total productive maintenance moves from an emphasis on simple repair to a focus on prevention of machine breakdown problems.

There are six parts to total productive maintenance:

Operator involvement

Equipment selection

Corrective maintenance

Preventive maintenance

Breakdown maintenance

Record keeping

Operator Involvement

The degree of operator involvement in TPM is quite high. It involves the operator becoming the early warning system as one part of preventive maintenance. It involves the operator being responsible for increasing portions of routine preventive maintenance, such as cleaning and lubricating. It involves the operator being part of the decision-making process in the selection of new or replacement equipment. Finally, it extends to an operator being able to handle more and more breakdown maintenance over time—from first aid-type things to more complex breakdown maintenance after proper training.

Equipment Selection

In addition to the operators being directly involved in the selection process, equipment selection would be based on life-cycle costing. Traditional selection is based on how efficient a machine is when it is running. Life-cycle costing considers maintenance costs and changeover costs adding up to overall costs over the life of the machine.

Corrective Maintenance

Corrective maintenance refers to modifying equipment, after it is received, to the particular application in that company, as well as the application of the concept of continuous improvement. If corrective maintenance is performed on equipment each year, the equipment should get better and more efficient each year. Traditional thinking says that equipment will deteriorate each year until it becomes unusable and must be replaced.

Preventive Maintenance

It should be clear in nearly everyone's mind what preventive maintenance is. But in a total productive maintenance environment, preventive maintenance is only one of six components of the larger picture.

Breakdown Maintenance

There are two main points to be made about breakdown maintenance.

One is the heavy level of operator involvement. In order to fulfill the requirements of operators becoming increasingly involved in breakdown maintenance, there must be a heavy training component. Operators must first be taught first aid techniques, and, over a period of time, more complex techniques of breakdown maintenance.

An insistence on permanently solving problems is the other side of breakdown maintenance. This is an attitude that always asks the question, What needs to be done so this breakdown never occurs again? This is a major part of the philosophy that over a period of time equipment will get better.

Record Keeping

The final component of total productive maintenance is record keeping. Operators are heavily involved in keeping records of problems, breakdowns, and costs. These records provide the basis for making decisions on selection of new equipment, by identifying what patterns of problems exist that require preventive maintenance and what patterns of problems warrant a redesign or improvement of a portion of the equipment.

It should be clear that total quality and Just In Time have a unique relationship. How far and how quickly a company can implement Just In Time is limited by the predictability of the process. For that reason, a total quality effort that brings predictability—not necessarily perfection—to the manufacturing process is often necessary before Just In Time can be implemented. But fortunately there is a reciprocal agreement; JIT makes the implementation of total quality much faster and easier.

THE NEW PARTNERSHIP: JIT AND MRP

As material requirements planning (MRP I) and then manufacturing resource planning (MRP II) have evolved in the United States since the 1960s, the more holistic approach of Just In Time has been developed by leading edge companies in Japan. Unfortunately, many people have seen MRP and JIT as being in competition and conflict. It is time to put the controversy to rest, understand what is really behind these two ideas, and recognize each as a valuable contribution to a coherent manufacturing strategy, and both as compatible concepts and techniques that can be put together to achieve even greater results than when used alone.

While the Japanese were putting the concepts of JIT into a coherent manufacturing strategy, the APICS society in the United States pulled together the disintegrated tools of its discipline—Reorder Point (ROP), Economical Order Quantity (EOQ), Material Requirement Planning (MRP; known now as MRP I), Distribution Requirement Planning (DRP), Capacity Requirement Planning (CRP), Shop Floor Control (SFC), and others—into a coherent planning, scheduling, and control strategy (MRP II).

But until JIT arrived on the Western scene, there was no manufacturing strategy to parallel and implement the rapid development of market and product strategies. As a result, there was no manufacturing framework on which to hang MRP II. Too many of the technical resource people made available to manufacturing have been technique-happy mechanics who view parts of the whole but fail to understand the complete subject and properly fit all the techniques and mechanics into a conceptual framework that can lead to the most cost-effective operation.

The conflict between MRP and Kanban (linking operations) is a case in point—specialists in scheduling arguing about techniques while failing to address the manufacturing process and understand when one or the other approach is desirable.

Some people argue that JIT should supersede MRP II. But MRP II should not be thrown out, rather it should be used more intelligently in relation to JIT. Much of it can be simplified from its original conception in job shops to fit with a JIT environment. MRP II represents the most thorough planning and scheduling strategy developed to date, and is a necessary complement to the implementation of a manufacturing strategy. In addition, many MRP II functions are required as bridges to a JIT environment.

Companies often ask if they should implement MRP before JIT or JIT before MRP, and if they are considering JIT should they implement MRP at all.

My feeling is that MRP and JIT complement each other very well. But remember, MRP wants to work with the scheduling process to do the best job possible, while JIT wants to radically alter the manufacturing process. Because of this, companies must consider why they want to implement either MRP or JIT, or both, before deciding in which order to do the implementation.

If a company is coming apart at the seams, my inclination is to say to implement MRP, both in order to get control and in order to keep the situation from deteriorating further by asking employees to make such a radical change as JIT.

But if the company is basically under control but looking for improvements, I would think about implementing the basics of JIT first. Then, the MRP system that needs to be implemented is vastly simplified and reduced in scope. This system will therefore take less time and expense to implement, and can assist in making the transition to a more complete JIT environment.

WHAT IS MANUFACTURING RESOURCES PLANNING?

The production and inventory control specialists in the United States focused on customer service and inventory control, and developed a comprehensive group of techniques between 1960 and 1975, with evolving computer assistance. These techniques were finally integrated into a planning and scheduling strategy for all types of manufacturing.

Manufacturing resource planning consists of three activities:

Demand management

Supply management

Capacity management

These activities are carried out in two phases—planning and execution.

The basic function of demand management is controlling sales forecasts and customer orders.

The basic function of supply management is controlling planning and scheduling at both the planning and execution phases. Supply management covers three levels of scheduling:

Production planning

Master scheduling

Material requirements planning (MRP I)

Supply management includes the control of the shop and vendors in meeting the schedules.

The basic function of capacity management is identifying and resolving capacity constraints within the planning and execution phases.

Figure 9.1 represents MRP II as a matrix of these functions, divided into planning and execution phases.

Most of these activities are missing in the writings on JIT, perhaps because they are assumed to be in place. However:

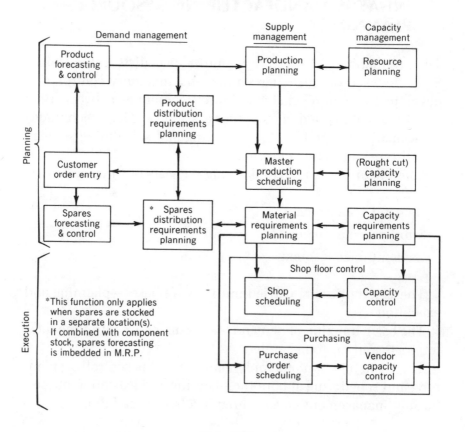

Figure 9.1.

Demand management is required for any manufacturing strategy, regardless of what scheduling system is used.

Likewise, every manufacturing operation must have a production plan and a master schedule.

Capacity planning is increasingly important to more closely synchronize the operations to the load placed on manufacturing by the master schedule.

The critical junction of planning and execution is the MRP I function. If MRP II is recognized as a planning strategy and JIT as an execution strategy, then MRP I becomes the JIT/MRP II junction.

There are six elements of MRP I:

On-hand balance

Lot sizing

Safety stock

Lead time

Gross requirements (demand plan)

Scheduled receipts/planned orders (supply plan)

Figure 9.2 shows a typical MRP I output, which, under the traditional MRP II concept is a material planning and scheduling system. It not only plans material requirements but also maintains the due date for each component supply order so that each order will arrive "just in time" for use by the next level—ultimately the end item scheduled by the master production schedule.

Under traditional MRP II concepts there are three levels of scheduling:

Master Schedule—quantity and date for completion of end items

Materials Requirement Planning—scheduling the completion

M.R.P. Output

Gross to net requirements planning—Lens assembly

OH = 30   SS = 10   LT = 4 weeks   CLT = 9 weeks   OQ = 4 periods

	Past Due	1	2	3	4	5	6	7	8
Dependent requirements				60				50	
Independent requirements		10	10	10	10	10	10	10	10
Gross requirements		10	10	70	10	10	10	60	10
Order receipt			*100				**（90）		
Projected available	20	10	100	30	20	10	90	30	20
Order release			（90）			100			

* ☐ Scheduled receipt ☐   ** ☐ Planned order ☐

Figure 9.2.

and start dates of the components and raw materials dependent on the master schedule

Shop Floor Control—scheduling the operations performed on a component between MRP start and finish dates; often called priority sequencing.

But under JIT, shop floor control is unnecessary, since parts go from start to completion in less than a day. Master scheduling is still required by JIT and, in fact, becomes more sophisticated. MRP I does not go away, but becomes progressively simpler.

The JIT approach involves a program dedicated to:

Eliminating on-hand by moving completed components directly to the next user without going in and out of stock

Eliminating lot sizing by reducing setup to the point where lot sizes of one generate no manufacturing cost (time) penalty

Eliminating safety stock by removing all causes for safety stock

Reducing lead time by speeding up throughput and eliminating causes for move and wait time

Smoothing out gross requirements by making only what is needed

Eliminating any difference between requirements (demand) and orders (supply) because of elimination of lot sizing and synchronization of production to the master schedule.

Figure 9.3 shows the MRP output after JIT has had its effect. Eliminating lot sizing at the master schedule level has smoothed out the dependent demand. The demand line (gross requirements) will be the same as the supply line (scheduled receipts), and "netting" and "net requirements" disappear.

As lead time disappears, MRP is too slow for scheduling, and linking operations—where operations schedule each other—takes over. Is MRP still needed?

Very much so. First, it will take years to achieve full effectiveness (Toyota took 15 years) and an effective scheduling methodology (MRP II) will be needed to bridge that time.

Where JIT can be fully applied, MRP becomes increasingly simplified and acts as the transition tool until its scheduling function disappears as linking operations becomes feasible. But even under full JIT production, the gross requirements generation, exploding the master production schedule through a bill of

MRP Output

Under J–I–T Production

Gross to net requirements planning—Lens assembly

OH = O   SS = O   LT = 1 day   CLT = 2 weeks   OQ = 1 piece

	Past Due	1	2	3	4	5	6	7	8
Dependent requirements		15	15	15	15	14	13	12	12
Independent requirements		10	10	10	10	10	10	10	10
Gross requirements		25	25	25	25	24	23	22	22

Figure 9.3.

material for the purpose of material planning (suppliers) and as input to capacity planning (manufacturing) will always be needed.

Also, MRP I was developed for job-shop manufacturing, whereas JIT was generated in a repetitive manufacturing environment. Some plants or products that have job-shop characteristics may never be suitable for the full application of JIT.

Any of the existing MRP software packages available today will require modification. A system will have to be able to think in terms of days or hours and will have to calculate lead times differently. They will have to work without shop orders and without stock rooms as control points. Another major capability they will have to have is the ability to distinguish JIT parts or products from not-yet JIT parts or products.

In order to integrate JIT production with MRP II, manufacturers will need to continue the planning activities that are part of MRP II.

When MRP II and JIT are jointly implemented, master scheduling will become more sophisticated. Material requirements planning will become simpler. In addition, shop floor control will become unnecessary. Remember, even perfect JIT will not eliminate the helpfulness of MRP.

10

JUST-IN-TIME IMPLEMENTATION: MANAGEMENT'S CRUCIAL ROLE

Now that we understand the technical elements of Just-In-Time manufacturing, the question is how to make JIT happen. Western companies are having a widely varying degree of success in their efforts to implement JIT. There are two major variables we at Rath and Strong see among companies we work with that spell the difference between complete success, partial success, and failure. One is the reason JIT is being implemented in a company. The other is whether or not the company takes a structured approach to the implementation process.

159

The most successful companies are trying to move to a JIT environment in order to meet external challenges: to gain or hold onto market share, increase quality, and lower price. These companies seek to make their manufacturing a strategic tool in the marketplace.

Other companies are thinking of JIT more along the lines of a tool to reduce costs, streamline the manufacturing process, and hence improve profit margins. These companies tend to be successful in implementing JIT, but noticeably less successful than those looking for a real manufacturing weapon.

The least successful companies are often thinking of JIT merely as a way to reduce inventories.

Why are companies that think of JIT as a way to make manufacturing a strategic tool more successful than other companies?

Because this rationale creates a much more positive atmosphere for everyone involved in the process. If the objective is advantage in the marketplace—in fact market growth by making manufacturing a strategic weapon—the benefits of JIT are more obvious and the climate is more positive to make it happen. If the reasons are reducing inventory and cutting costs, people often feel that their job security and status are threatened.

In terms of structure, we recommend a specific, structured approach to implementing JIT, a three-phase, six-step approach that starts the entire process off by reaching a decision as to why JIT is being implemented. We call this phase, which deals with the all-important question of why, the preparation phase.

From there, the process goes on to define how the implementation process will be structured and managed. We call this the organization phase. Finally, the process is a guide for successful step-by-step implementation by carrying out pilot projects, and, later, for project-by-project implementation, for education, and, finally, for the changing of company systems and norms—getting the company to a point where the JIT philosophy is a permanent way of life. We call this the implementation and institutionalization phase.

THE THREE PHASES OF JIT IMPLEMENTATION

The First Phase: Getting To Why

A basic question facing every leader embarking on Just In Time must be: How can this convert manufacturing in this company into a strategic tool that will enhance market position? The question should not be: How can this cut costs?

In this first phase of implementing JIT, the company needs to develop the specific reason why it is embarking on JIT. This is done by developing a set of visions of what the company could be like working in a JIT environment, then seeing how those visions can be incorporated into a company strategy to get ahead of competition in the marketplace, and how vision and strategy can be shared with the entire organization.

There are two steps in this phase. The first is awareness, the second strategy. (See Figures 10.1 through 10.3.)

8 In the awareness step, senior management needs to develop a detailed enough understanding of JIT to form a series of three interconnected visions of the future:

A physical vision

A climate vision

A marketplace vision

For the physical vision, senior management should be able to put together a picture of what the company could and should look like three to five years ahead in terms of the physical layout of manufacturing and the flow of materials through the purchasing, manufacturing, and distribution processes. This vision must be specific enough to be quantified; senior management should be able to answer such questions as:

What current wastes will be eliminated?

Which of my costs will be lowered and by how much?

How will the product flow?

Where will there be machine cells, pull systems, etc.?

What will setup times be?

What will throughput times be?

How many key suppliers will there be?

How frequently will they deliver?

With what lead times will they deliver?

What items will be delivered directly to the point of use?

How fast will customer orders be filled?

What products will we be able to produce every day, every two days, every week?

The climate vision is a vision of what the company's climate will have to be like in order to make JIT a reality.

In the marketplace vision, top management must convert its quantified physical vision to a mental picture of a set of potential opportunities in the marketplace, opportunities to get a jump on the competition. These include:

Faster delivery

More frequent deliveries

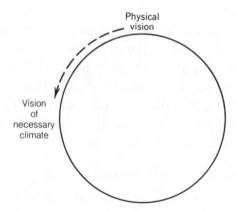

Figure 10.1.

Better customer service

More product variety

Lower price

Better quality

Next, the company must make the transition from these visions into a coherent strategy for selectively developing its potentials. The company must think through which of the capabilities it will acquire under JIT can be used in the marketplace, and which capabilities are most important to which customers or which markets.

Finally, the company must develop the visions into a specific strategy of manufacturing and market-share growth. This strategy needs to be explainable to people at all levels of the organization in terms that are meaningful to them.

One level will be concerned with growth and expansion. Another level will be concerned with changing responsibilities and job status.

Another level will be concerned with job security.

If this strategy is the right one for the company, it can drive the required changes and create the kind of climate necessary to insure that the physical and technical aspects of JIT actually take place.

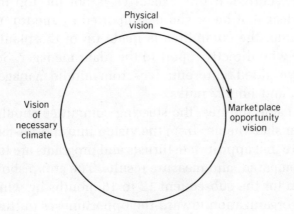

Figure 10.2.

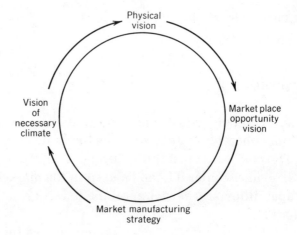

Figure 10.3.

The Second Phase: Creating The Structure

Once the vision and strategy have been developed, the second phase—organization—can begin to take shape. There are four key players involved in organization—the steering committee, a facilitator, project teams, and project team leaders.

1. It is important to establish a steering committee, chaired by a senior executive. It this executive is not the top manager it must be clear that he or she is supported by the top manager's power. Often, the committee is made up of the plant manager and those who directly report to the plant manager. Some companies have added representatives from middle management, supervisory, and hourly ranks.

As the name implies, the steering committee should steer. It should translate themes from the vision into shorter-term priorities, ensure that appropriate thrusts and programs are formulated and implemented, and measure results. The group should establish a plan for the subsequent 12 to 18 months by which it will guide the organization toward the opportunities outlined in the JIT assessment.

2. The facilitator must be a trusted and visible person whose primary responsibility is to ensure that the JIT effort moves along and that both the short- and long-term objectives are achieved. This facilitator is empowered by senior management to make sure JIT gets off to a solid and successful start.

Because of the unique role this person is to play, he or she must have certain characteristics, such as the ability to get something started, let others influence it and move it ahead, and not worry about getting the credit.

3. Project teams must be created to run each one of the pilots, then each one of the projects in the project-by-project implementation of JIT. Each project team should have a clear charter that defines its task in the JIT implementation. The teams must be made up of members of senior and middle management as well as shop-floor employees—those who will be carrying out the change.

Each team should have a specific, narrowly defined goal to change a technique or solve a problem. Initial projects should be chosen that give the team the greatest learning experience and the most potential for success. If the project can have a significant return on the time and energy invested, and address a pressing need, all the better.

4. Team leaders need to act both as the team's staff and its liaison with the steering committee. Although the teams will usually only meet once a week for a couple of hours, the leader must be able to devote another six or so hours to getting work done for the team so its next meeting can be productive, and so that the process can be kept moving.

The Third Phase: Putting The Plan Into Action

The first two phases of the JIT process must be driven by the most senior executive. Responsibility cannot be delegated. In this third phase, however, it is a different story. As the steering committee takes hold and carries out its mission, the remaining phase of JIT implementation will be put in place. In this remaining phase the role of top management changes. Here top management must guide rather than direct, facilitate rather than drive, as people throughout the organization begin to make the effort their own.

The third phase has three steps:

Pilot projects and project-by-project implementation

Education—broadening knowledge about JIT and making use of pilot and project successes

Institutionalization

Project-by-project implementation typically starts with pilot efforts to install particular JIT techniques. Setup reduction, machine cells, and pull systems are typical pilot opportunities because, depending on the situation, dramatic results can be achieved in a relatively short period of time by using new techniques.

Other pilots could also revolve around external areas of opportunity such as JIT purchasing, or nonmanufacturing opportunities such as paperwork processes. There are criteria for pilots and a process for choosing them. Pilots should balance the need for learning in a controlled environment with the ability to guarantee success for those involved in the pilots and the possibility of achieving significant results.

Training should be taking place while the pilots are going on to help employees develop the skills they need to carry JIT forward. This on-the-job training enables employees to see and feel what it takes to make JIT a reality.

UNSTRUCTURED APPROACH

Companies too undisciplined or too impatient to take a structured approach will often jump right into pilot projects. Even if such pilots are technically successful, there are two major dangers in not having a structured approach.

The first danger is that the pilots have not been shown to be a part of the overall strategy. They will be seen merely as a cost-cutting tool by those involved and may antagonize many of the shop-floor employees who are key to making JIT work.

The second danger is that without a vision a company will be satisfied with Just In Time in its cost-cutting role and will leave 85 percent of the real opportunity behind.

The education step should begin once pilots are underway and employees can see results beginning to emerge. Education should be tailored to a particular company's needs. All employees should be exposed to specially designed seminars on those particular facets of JIT most appropriate for their own company.

The final step involves actions to institutionalize Just In Time. Institutionalization means ensuring that people act in accordance with JIT principles over time. This requires adapting the organization's central systems—information systems, reward systems, and measurement systems. If this phase is not successful, there is a danger of JIT being short-lived. Much of the gains will be lost if, for example, the cost system continues to measure speed of machines rather than whether the machines are being utilized to produce what the customer wants when he wants it. Similarly, if the reward system encourages individual activity at the expense of group collaboration and teamwork, JIT will not last.

This also means adapting the norms of the business, those value statements and policies that tend to encourage or discourage specific behaviors, so that they are consistent with the principles of JIT.

LINES AND CIRCLES

In the early days of working out this three-phase, six-step process for implementing Just In Time, I thought of it as a linear process. One phase had to be completed before the next one began. But I quickly ran into a problem with this mental graphic.

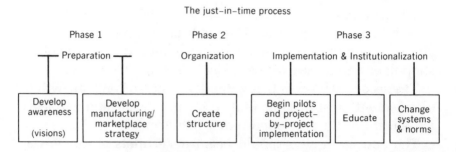

Figure 10.4.   The Just-In-Time Process

There are two major reasons why the linear picture of JIT implementation does not suffice. (See Figure 10.4.)

One is that a linear progression implies that at the end the process has been finished. With JIT, that is not the case. The JIT ideal of constant improvement does not only hold true in a physical process that JIT deals with. It also holds true for the implementation process.

Remember that the education and institutionalization steps are really the awareness step for the next generation of the company's employees being brought into the JIT process.

Notice that at the end of the sixth step—institutionalization—I said that one of the goals is to get more people within the organization thinking about how JIT can affect company strategy. If that is successfully done, then the next stage in the process becomes strategy again.

After the strategy is reexamined, the steering committee and project leader (who more often than not will still be in place) can implement another round of projects (although they may not be called pilot projects). Education will probably be ongoing, at least for a while, and the results of the next group of projects can be incorporated into the education. Changes brought about by these projects also must be institutionalized. Then it is back to awareness and strategy.

In effect, the process is circular, almost like a pinwheel (see Figure 10.5). After the pinwheel's first revolution, awareness is spun off. After three or four revolutions, the education phase

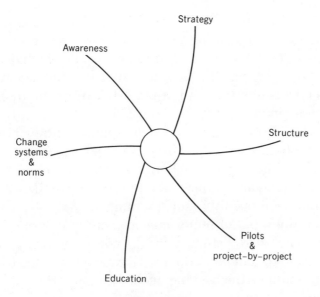

Figure 10.5.

may have been completed and also spun off. The organization will be in place in some way or another, and will be a semitransparent piece of the process. But the pinwheel will continue to revolve, from strategy to projects and training to institutionalization of the benefits of the last project efforts and back to strategy again.

Whether the process is seen as a linear or circular one, the point to emphasize is that there is a process. Although there is not one particular way to carry out each of the three phases and six steps, it is necessary to set up a formal mechanism and to follow the process. The process provides wholeness and continuity to JIT implementation.

If the process is not followed, there are a number of pitfalls a company can fall into.

Although Rath and Strong, as a consulting firm, might enter the picture for a company at any phase of the implementation process, we always go back to phase one and check to make sure all of the steps have been taken. Too often, companies rush willy-nilly into Just In Time without thinking through all of the implications.

Often, a company official, after obtaining minimal awareness of JIT through a seminar or conference, will come back and sell management on the concept. But in our result-oriented Western manufacturing world, the first step that new JIT champion is asked to take is to set up a pilot project. This short-circuiting of the process almost always leads to failure.

First, the pilot project bucks up against entrenched ideas about manufacturing on the part of both management and hourly personnel. Without giving JIT a chance to percolate and pass through the company grapevine, a pilot project will only be disruptive and face hostility and resentment.

Without the input of senior management in determining how JIT fits into an overall strategy for the company, many in senior management will not buy into the JIT concept, and the JIT champion will not have the backing needed from up the ladder to be able to push JIT in.

TOP MANAGEMENT'S ROLE

In all discussions of JIT, few deal with the specific role of top management in successful JIT implementation. A strong CEO, divisional vice-president, general manager, vice-president of manufacturing, or other top manager is the most effective force behind the JIT movement. Whatever the title, the movement for a successful JIT program must come from the top decision maker in the organization being converted to JIT.

Because so many JIT ideas run counter to traditionally accepted Western manufacturing notions, implementation can cause tremendous stress that crosses departmental lines. Ideally, the top manager will be above that stress, and thus be able to create bridges and connections to deal with it.

On a very basic level, employees often are reluctant to change the way they have been doing things for years. They are comfortable with old ways. Under the surface may be a fear of failure that goes along with being asked to try something new. The fear that new business practices will jeopardize their jobs—possibly even make them obsolete—is also very real. And especially in the United States, where individuality is valued so highly, supervisors and managers often resist the cross-department coordination practices that are crucial to the success of Just-In-Time manufacturing.

The climate necessary for successful JIT implementation is made up of four parts:

Strong leadership from the CEO (or other top management official)

A companywide ethic that encourages innovation and enables employees to feel that they can really make a difference

Teamwork within departments at all levels of the business, as well as cooperation between departments

People whose skills are matched to the needs of their jobs and who are driven to make their company better

This climate enables the CEO to put in place the various elements necessary for JIT success. If a company is working from such a base, it will be able to do what is required to solve problems, to train people in new methods, to educate them in new concepts, and to institutionalize the new ways of doing things.

Perhaps the most important attribute for the top executive in leading a JIT effort is how he or she thinks about the task of revitalizing manufacturing and gets others to think about it. One part of this task is behavior. Leaders must behave in a way that is a model for how others should act. As much as anything, getting the most from JIT means training and encouraging people to incessantly question traditional practices and ways of thinking. In order for this to happen, leaders must question present practices through both words and deeds, thereby indicating to others that it is acceptable to do so.

In the next three chapters, I will develop each of the three phases in greater detail, using the methodology we have developed at Rath and Strong for taking a structured approach to developing a coherent transition to a JIT environment.

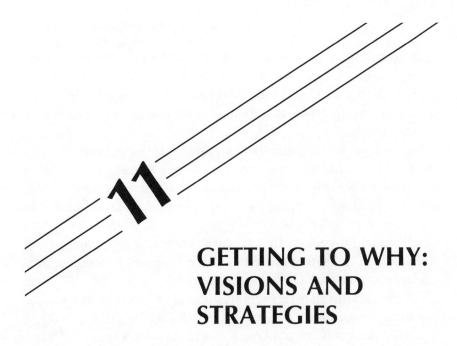

GETTING TO WHY: VISIONS AND STRATEGIES

The goal in preparing to implement Just In Time is to get a company to a point where top management is driving the change and where the entire work force knows the reason or reasons why change is needed. In order to properly prepare, a company's top management needs to have a vision of what the company will look like under Just In Time and how Just In Time can help the company either increase or hold its own in the market. In short, until top management has created a business strategy that incorporates Just In Time, it is difficult to communicate the need for JIT to the general work force.

Much of the preparation for JIT is similar to that of any other

large-scale planned change. JIT is, after all, a philosophy that requires people to develop different attitudes and behaviors. Any
change of this sort is liable to be resisted if those pushing the
change imply that previous behavior and attitudes were wrong
or inadequate.

Many behavioral scientists contend that if change is to occur it
must be preceded by an unfreezing of the current climate that
provides the basis for current behavior and attitudes. Kent Lewin
used the analogy over 30 years ago of making something that is
presently in a solid state into a liquid state so that the whole
thing can be moved. As this process evolves, it is crucial for top
management to keep in mind that there is, in any unfreezing process, the threat that change represents.

For something like JIT, which depends so much on people's
commitment and on a change in thinking leading to a change in
behavior, this threat could potentially destroy any JIT effort.

There are a number of roadblocks that will naturally be
thrown in the way of JIT implementation. During the preparation
phase, top management must acknowledge these roadblocks and
begin to formulate responses to them. Among these roadblocks
are:

1. *Measurement, reward, and information systems.* Top management can say anything they want to say about quality, balance, and small lots, but if the day-to-day measurement and reward system doesn't change, if machines are still measured by
speed, and negative variances are sent to lines that are in balance
yet running slowly, behavior will not change.

Similarly, the information system must support JIT. If top
management is saying one thing about measures and what needs
to be measured, but if other measurements continue to be made
and decisions are made based on these measurements, the company runs the risk of JIT being short-lived.

2. *Inflexibility of work practices.* Job descriptions and work
practices often run counter to successful implementation of JIT
and pose a difficult issue in organizing a JIT implementation. A
very important distinction to make here is that we are not talking

about the work force being innately inflexible. If people's behavior is inflexible, it is usually for some reason. More often than not, we find that the practices and rules under which people are asked to operate are inflexible.

3. *The strategy of the business itself.* If the business' strategy is internal—built on clinging to what it has and increasing profit—the focus of attention in implementing a JIT effort will be different from what is required for JIT to be really successful. Having the proper focus—a focus on the marketplace—is essential to ensuring that the business' strategy is consistent with a JIT philosophy.

4. *The organization's climate.* Simply put, JIT will not work if the company's climate encourages behavior that hinders teamwork, discourages people from identifying problems and offering new ideas. The company's climate is one of the most important variables in JIT implementation. It must be measured and, where necessary, changed.

Another aspect of the climate that must be assessed is whether JIT is seen as being just another project. Many JIT efforts we have been asked to assess after they have turned in poor or mediocre results have had a project of the month quality to them. This problem is very specifically a reflection of top management's lack of ability to institute change and manage transition.

5. *Motivation.*–This is especially important to middle managers. Top managers will often be motivated by what they see as the potential bottom-line results of their newly developed manufacturing strategy. But middle managers have more pressing personal questions about JIT, such as what it means to their job security, prestige, influence, and salary.

GETTING IT TO THE TOP

More often than not, awareness of JIT enters a company organization below the top level of management, often through an operations department. Initial interest in JIT most often enters a company at the level of the materials manager, the vice-president of manufacturing, or the company's productivity guru, whatever his or her title may be.

Whatever level it comes in at, JIT must get up to the top decision maker as fast as possible. If it does, there is a good chance senior management will understand the possibilities and implications and incorporate JIT into a corporate strategy for growth and change. If, however, JIT flourishes at the upper-middle-management level, yet does not get fully accepted at the top level, the danger is that implementation will be left to those in the upper-middle level, who don't have the power or position to overcome the inevitable roadblocks to JIT implementation.

There are a number of ways in which those responsible for bringing JIT into the company can get it to the top quickly, including:

Get the top person to go to a JIT seminar run by people with a solid track record in JIT implementation.

Arrange meetings with or visits to companies that have successfully implemented JIT and make sure people from those companies are at the same level as the managers listening to them.

Bring someone in from the outside to conduct a data-gathering session, give the executive an overview of JIT and some ideas of what JIT can do for the company.

After helping senior management develop an initial awareness of JIT, it is time to sit back. The next move is up to the top manager.

Many people responsible for introducing JIT to a company have tried to run a pilot project or two to show the top manager just how powerful JIT is. This has many dangers for backfiring.

One danger is that the pilot will be too narrow and will not show the kind of results that are truly possible, deflating the argument.

Another danger is running into dissent from the shop floor or middle-level supervisors that not only defeats the JIT project, but causes lasting disagreements between management and hourly workers.

In one instance, a plant manager of a major U.S. electronics firm decided to try a machine cell pilot to prove to his management that JIT would succeed. He followed the book technically, but paid no attention to the climate and employee involvement aspects that can make or break a project such as this. Confusion, missed schedules, and a dip in product quality caused embarrassment and cost significant dollars and precious time in getting the pilot project, and the plant, back on track.

In another instance, an upper-middle-level manager who introduced JIT to his company set up a machine cell pilot project in one of many company product lines. Just as he was about to announce his great success, the product line was sold to another company.

LET'S GET STARTED

Assuming the top manager has said, "Let's make JIT happen here," it is time to seriously begin the preparation phase.

This phase has to do with developing three visions of what the company will look like in the future—a physical vision, a climate vision, and a marketplace vision. Then these three visions must be developed into a strategy. Finally, the visions and strategy must be shared with the entire organization.

At this stage, the top manager has to get his key people together to develop these visions.

One of the most important bases to cover at this point is participation and a sense of involvement on the part of leaders from every function. Some companies make the mistake of letting JIT be solely a manufacturing effort. This is as dangerous as letting the business strategy be developed without taking into account manufacturing needs and capabilities, which many companies did prior to the 1980s.

Marketing, finance, human resources, sales, engineering, quality, materials, MIS, and research and development each have a major stake in JIT, and must be intimately involved in its formulation. This means they must be a part of the development of the company's visions and strategy.

Physical Vision

This group must develop its knowledge of JIT to a significantly higher degree than was necessary to simply motivate the top manager. They need a thorough enough understanding of each JIT technique in order to brainstorm where and how they can utilize these techniques in their own company. They need to ask themselves such questions as:

1. What current wastes will be eliminated? Each JIT technique is designed to eliminate waste in the manufacturing process. It is necessary to see how the pieces all fit together, and where all the wastes will be eliminated by implementing JIT. A corollary to this question is: Which costs will be lowered and by how much?

2. How will the product flow? People need to look into the specifics of where machine cells will be, or pull systems. The actual setup times and throughput times must be determined.

3. How many key suppliers will there be? Frequency of delivery, lead times of deliveries, and what items will be delivered directly to the point of use need to be considered.

4. How fast will customer orders be filled?

And finally, the manufacturing timetable should be clear: what products a company will be able to produce every day, every two days, or every week.

In order to do this, seeing is better than reading, so in addition to attending seminars and reading books, top executives should visit companies where JIT is being successfully utilized. Japan is still the most impressive place to go to see the cutting edge of JIT. But a number of U.S. companies can serve as good models—even if they have not incorporated all of the JIT elements. In a second round of seminars, visits, and discussions, the presentations should go into far greater detail than in the early stages of making the top executive aware of JIT. The team may want to split the task up and make team members specialists in one JIT technique or another.

The most useful tool for developing a vision of what the physical process ought to look like is the value-added test.

The team should go onto its own manufacturing floor and do a value-added test. Take a bread-and-butter product and follow it through the entire manufacturing process. Don't simply get a routing sheet and read what is supposed to happen to the product. Physically follow the path the product takes.

Start with a raw material or a major component arriving at the receiving dock. Follow it through the physical process, writing down every activity that happens to it—everywhere it moves, everywhere it waits, every pair of hands that touch it. Continue this through until a finished product is being shipped to a customer.

Once this list of activities is available, each activity needs to be tested with two questions. First: Does the activity directly add value to the product? Second: Is it being done right the first time?

Every activity that fails either of these two tests is a waste and becomes a candidate for elimination through the various JIT techniques or by solving quality problems.

Now that a list of non-value-adding activities has been targeted for elimination, the team has to think in specific enough terms to decide which technique would best be used to eliminate which wastes.

The process must be considered as a whole before it is broken up into component parts and those parts are considered individually for action. Frequently, by looking at an entire batch-oriented process it is seen that there are duplicate steps that could be eliminated by minor changes in prior steps, or that by changing an early step somewhere later steps become unnecessary.

The next step is to look for where it is possible to get to the ultimate goal—one-at-a-time production:

By dedicating and relocating equipment

By running equipment at the speeds required

By reducing set-up times

When operations are performed very closely together a number of steps disappear, such as:

Cleaning

Sorting into priorities

Inspecting

Weigh counting

For instance, setting up a work cell often eliminates a number of inspection and cleaning steps that have been built into the process on the assumption that the batches will sit around. The cleaning is to get rid of the accumulated dust and dirt. The inspection is necessary because the goods will not be used immediately. With a work cell and one-at-a-time production, the parts don't sit around—end of cleaning step—and in continuous production, following operations constitute 100 percent inspection of prior operations—end of separate inspection step.

There will, however, be a number of times when it will be impossible to get to one-at-a-time production. Maybe it is impossible to dedicate machines because of the wide variety of product being made. Maybe equipment is too large to move. Maybe there is a problem with reliability—too much machine downtime. Maybe there is a quality problem that needs to be solved first.

When the ultimate goal of one-at-a-time production is not yet possible, the team should consider second-choice JIT techniques, particularly pull systems. A pull system will always reduce some of the inventory and cut out some of the non-value-adding steps, and the indirect labor and other costs associated with them.

The team must be specific in its thinking. It must decide which problems are solvable in three to five years—reliability and quality should be—and which problems are not solvable—size, mobility, and variety of product may not be.

In the first part of the material flow, a number of steps could be eliminated through JIT purchasing—incoming inspection, handling, counting, paperwork, changing containers, and moving in and out of storerooms. If there is a large number of suppliers and constantly changing suppliers, there is almost inevitably a large number of non-value-adding steps necessary to control the constantly changing environment.

It is a judgment call how many product lines need to undergo the process to determine the vision. Some companies want to do this exercise with every line, while others do it on one or two and extrapolate those results over all other lines.

A detailed picture must be created, both graphically and in words, of what the manufacturing process could look like under JIT three to five years out. Determine what the process would look like in terms of space, inventory, direct and indirect labor, overhead (including salaried people), and response time to customers.

Climate Vision

A by-product of the detailed thinking about how the workplace will look leads to the second vision necessary for successful implementation of JIT: a vision of what the climate needs to be in order to make the necessary changes over the three-to-five-year time frame. There are three main areas that need to be explored:

1. Work force flexibility

   Job descriptions, work practices

   Cross training

   Working in teams rather than individually

2. Employee involvement

   Self-inspection

Problem solving (team approach)

Continuous improvement

3. Teamwork

Risk taking, willingness to experiment

Cooperation across departmental lines

In addition, there must be a recognition that a mix of skills will be needed so that people's job content can be changed. Employees will need to be willing and able to learn new skills, and employers need to be willing and able to help employees learn these skills. As a corollary to this, measurement and reward systems must be changed.

Marketplace Vision

The third vision the company needs to develop is the marketplace vision. In this vision, the team must determine what the opportunities will be, given vision of the new manufacturing capabilities of the company, to meet customer requirements better than in the past and to meet customer requirements the company was unable to meet in the past. Some of the ways the new manufacturing capabilities will help the company are:

Faster delivery because of the company's shortened, simplified manufacturing process, and having reduced lead times from suppliers through JIT purchasing.

More frequent deliveries and smaller quantities because of reduced setup times.

Better customer service in terms of quality and meeting delivery promises because of streamlined manufacturing process, problem solving, and a habit of doing it right the first time.

Increased product variety because of reduced setup times and the flexibility of pull systems.

Lower price because of elimination of waste activities.

Better quality because of immediate feedback, problem solving, and the habit of doing it right the first time.

DEVELOPING OPPORTUNITIES INTO A STRATEGY

After developing the physical vision leading to the vision of technical and theoretical JIT opportunities available to be used in the marketplace, it is time to sort out those opportunities and determine which ones could fit into the specifics of a strategy for the future. Companies need to determine which of the opportunities truly mean something in the marketplace; is the marketplace sensitive to response time, cost, price, or other factors?

The answer is often different depending on whether the company is trying to protect market share or go out and get new market share.

The issues most frequently important to keeping old customers are quality and reliable delivery. New customers are often attracted by price and short lead times.

Companies also often find that the answer is different for different product lines. Some lines are shipped off the shelf, so a reduction in lead time, even of 80 percent, means nothing. In another line, that reduction could take weeks off the published lead time and provide an immediate advantage over competition. For some product lines price is simply not the issue; but in other product lines price will directly relate to taking market share away from competitors.

Some markets are sensitive to minimum charges. Reducing setup times by 75 percent or more would practically eliminate these minimum charges and reduce the quantity level at which a company could offer price breaks. Some markets are sensitive to payment terms or other forms of positive cash flow. In such a case, a company will find that it can use cash flow from reduced inventory to offer longer payment terms. This increases accounts receivable, but in effect simply turns one accounting asset (inventory) into another asset (receivables) that means more in the marketplace.

STRATEGY SELLS

Having a specific strategy that tells what markets the company is going after with what tools and techniques and how the company will grow is a major enabler for selling JIT to all levels of the organization. With employees of each level, details of the visions must be used that mean something to them. This can only be done if the team has done a sufficiently detailed analysis of the company and what it would be like under JIT.

Essentially, there are two strategies into which JIT can be incorporated. One is a growth strategy, where JIT is being used to increase the share of an existing market or to develop new market niches or meet market needs better. The second strategy is survival—maintaining current market share or trying to stop erosion of market share.

If a company is truly in a survival mode, it must be honest with its employees. JIT must be understood as a necessary restructuring in a time of retrenchment. With or without JIT, the company's work force will probably shrink. But JIT gives the company its chance to survive as a leaner, more efficient business.

In a growth strategy, corporate leaders can justifiably stress —or ideally even guarantee—that the job losses from successful implementation of JIT will be offset by job gains from attracting a larger market share and increasing sales.

For the rest of this chapter, I will assume a strategy of growth, the best possible world in which to be implementing JIT.

Even with a growth strategy, top management needs to change the climate of a company to accept the changes JIT will bring about. To do this, top management must understand what motivates people at each level of the organization and what specific portions of this vision and strategy relate most directly to their concerns, enabling them to buy in to the plan.

ROADBLOCKS

Any kind of substantial change will be met with a number of roadblocks. That is only human nature. But having a coherent set of visions and strategy will enable the top management team to eliminate or, at least, minimize these roadblocks.

Many times guarantees must be made to the work force. The company that can guarantee the most security and stability to the work force during the JIT implementation will have the fewest problems with implementation.

Motivation

Perhaps the major roadblock to any organizational change is motivation. At each level of the organization, questions about change are different and approaches to motivation will be different.

Top managers are already motivated by what they see as JIT's strategic possibilities.

Middle management and first-line supervisors are motivated by an entirely different set of questions and needs. They must believe senior management truly wants these changes implemented, and that senior management is aware of middle management's problems and is willing to assist them in solving those problems. Middle managers feel threatened not only by the issue of job security but by the questions that revolve around job status. They want to know what their job will be, how they will function, and what their power will be. Middle managers are often not as vocal about their fears as members of the shop-floor work force, preferring to trust senior management yet allowing doubts to nag at them. There are five questions that are upper-most in the minds of middle managers:

1. How will this change the role of the middle manager in terms of importance and prestige? For example, if one change is going to be that operators will do their own inspections and there will be no inspectors, what will happen to today's supervisors and managers of inspection?

2. Does employee involvement undercut middle management and make middle managers look weak?

3. Do the middle managers have the flexibility to learn new skills and change their method of operating from telling people what to do to harnessing employee involvement—from overseer to coach? Senior management must agree to help middle managers develop and refine these skills.

4. Are the people who work for the middle manager or the supervisor going to learn skills that the managers themselves have not learned? Managers need to learn these skills.

5. Are the miracles ascribed to JIT truly doable in my area? Or is management going to come down hard if specific things turn out not to be technically feasible?

These middle managers need to have enough knowledge of the nuts and bolts of JIT so that they are not constantly afraid of being put in the middle—having employees angry at them for pushing things that are technically not possible, and senior management angry at them for not being able to do things.

For the shop floor, a common block to motivation is the issue of job security; as soon as shop-floor employees begin to be exposed to JIT they quickly understand that it means more can be done with less and their question becomes: Why should I take part in a program that will increase productivity and could cost me my job? Management must have a vision of growth in order to provide a positive yet honest answer in a clear and concise manner.

The work force should be asked to enter into a partnership with management for the good of the company—a partnership that can only be created by management. Management must also be willing to make an agreement and live up to it. If the strategy is one of growth, the trade-off between higher productivity and greater market share should be explained clearly.

If possible, a no-layoff guarantee should be made. Any decrease in the work force should be allowed to come about through attrition. Changes in the types of skills required should be handled through a retraining strategy.

If a vision of the company five years from now is that operators will do their own setups, what happens to today's setup people? They can be retrained to become maintenance technicians or toolroom specialists.

If another vision is that operators will do their own inspections, what will happen to today's inspectors? They can become quality assurance specialists working either with operators on prevention techniques or with suppliers to eliminate the need for incoming inspections.

Only by management making a commitment to workers will the company be able to gain the level of commitment on the part of workers to become flexible and change old work rules and practices.

Measurements and Rewards

While inappropriate measurements and rewards have a negative influence on shop-floor employees, by far the greatest effect is on middle managers. Top management can talk to middle managers until doomsday about new principles and new ways to operate, but if the measurement system doesn't change, middle managers' behavior will not change.

Such measurements as machine utilization, how busy people are, and how much is being produced without regard to need must be ended before middle management will really believe that senior management is trying to change the company.

Senior management cannot just tell middle managers, supervisors, and line workers to disregard measurements—the measurement must be suspended, at least during the running of pilot projects. In most instances, senior management will have to agree to stop certain measurements without knowing what other measurements will take their place.

This takes guts!

It is antithetical to traditional management. The only thing that can give management the confidence to suspend measurements is having a strategy that it knows is for the good of the company and will lead to growth.

Management's Track Record

It is important for senior management to know before implementing JIT what middle management and the shop-floor employees think about senior management's record of ability to direct change. The perception of this ability is very different at different levels of the organization.

If either middle management or the shop floor has been subjected to a history of inconsistencies from above, JIT implementation will face a rocky road.

JIT must be put in place in such a way that there is no doubt about management's long-term commitment, no chance for it to be seen as just another project of the month. If, for instance, management got very excited about a new way of doing things—say total quality—but the first time there was a crunch management said, "Ship it, anyway," very quickly the shop floor would get the message that, contrary to all the hoopla, quality is not the first priority; shipping is the first priority, quality is second.

This hurts middle management the most, since they are squeezed between the need to do senior management's bidding and the ill will the decision has generated with those who actually produce the goods.

If management has done this in the past, employees will be

waiting to see if management sends these mixed messages again with JIT.

This roadblock, too, can be effectively dealt with only if there is a credible and coherent set of visions and a strategy that is credible to the work force and gives management the strength of purpose it needs to keep the message consistent, even through periods of pressure.

If all steps are handled with care, what should emerge from this process is a vision and strategy that is realistic, workable, and that will obviously benefit the company's entire work force and, perhaps most of all, its customers.

12

ORGANIZING THE COMPANY FOR JIT

Once the preparation for a change to a Just-In-Time environment has occurred, it is necessary for the company to go through a number of organizational steps to successfully implement JIT. We suggest an approach that utilizes a steering committee to direct the company's JIT implementation efforts, and task forces or task groups to implement JIT pilot projects, such as setup reductions, machine cells, or pull systems.

This type of structure can be successful in managing any kind of major change. A number of companies have used the process when implementing total quality. Others have incorporated this design into their plans for conducting, and taking action on results from, an organization climate study. These changes often necessitate employing nontraditional methods in order to develop interdisciplinary cooperation in problem solving.

In this chapter, we will discuss the process in generic terms and in its specific applications to the massive changes required to move to a Just-In-Time manufacturing environment.

There are four key players in the management of a planned change such as JIT.

1. *Steering committee.* The steering committee must assess the implementation issues and obstacles involved in implementing a change, then develop an implementation strategy and plan to overcome the obstacles. It must select, sponsor, and facilitate task force teams, guide and troubleshoot for the task force teams in their implementation, and act on task force recommendations or conclusions. The steering committee is also responsible for the overall communication of task force activities; among task forces, from task forces to top management, and from task forces to the general company population.

2. *Facilitator.* It is important that the JIT-implementation project have a facilitator, someone with full-time or nearly full-time responsibility for making sure that the implementation takes place. This person is almost like the executive secretary of the steering committee, a nonvoting administrator, admiral's aide, chief of staff, and one-person legwork team.

3. *Task force team.* It is the goal of each task force team to make sure the implementation of its piece of JIT actually occurs. The team first must clarify its charter, scope, and objectives; identify and recommend project priorities; and determine how the implementation will be documented and presented to the steering committee and senior management.

4. *Task force leaders.* Task force leaders serve a task force as a project manager to help plan, organize, delegate, coordinate, and document the work of the task force. Often it is the task force leader who communicates with the steering committee to keep it appraised of the task force's progress.

THE STEERING COMMITTEE

Often in a JIT implementation the steering committee will be made up of some members of the company's top management team and powerful representatives from other levels in the company. Participation in the guiding group will often mean the difference between widespread support and resistance to change. However, the steering committee should not get much larger than eight people.

If the steering committee is made up of senior management, it gives the committee the advantage of already having done the preparation and understanding the reasons for change, the goals of the change, the vision of the company after the change, and the roadblocks that stand in the way of change. In effect, an entire level of communication and education is eliminated by not having to have senior management convince a steering committee of these points.

At the same time, however, the fact that members of the top team must orient others on a steering committee who did not go through the process of vision clarification can be very positive. It enables top managers to exert influence in an environment that is often more likely to produce agreement than in the normal course of day-to-day events. It also makes the job of influencing employees at large easier if people from various organizational levels who have their own constituencies are convinced that top management is committed to JIT for the right reasons.

One thing steering committees must be especially wary of if the committee is similar in composition to the senior management staff, is that members not behave during the steering committee meetings as they may do during staff meetings.

While it is not realistic—or advisable—to expect people to act completely differently once they are members of the JIT steering committee, dissent is vital for the steering of a JIT effort. If the top team is not used to open discussion, challenging existing ideas, and constructively confronting long-held views, it is likely that there will not be enough dissent; and without the right kind and amount of dissent the right decisions will not be made.

This is a critically important principle of the management of planned change. The leader's teamwork skills come into play here moreso than at any other juncture in the JIT implementation process.

Often the real breakthroughs in JIT efforts are a result of people on the steering committee learning to operate in a different way than is usual. At the same time, it is rarely necessary for people to act 180 degrees differently from the way they normally do. The point is that implementation of something as complex as JIT carries with it the need for different ways of operating on the part of everyone, and the steering committee is no exception. Its members must have the ability to work together as a team and deal effectively with conflict, allowing it to surface and managing it effectively. The CEO, as the primary leader of the company and the head of the steering committee, must ensure that this happens.

The chartering and training of a steering committee is the first of seven steps involved in the organizational phase of this structured approach to implementing JIT. The seven steps are:

1. Organize the steering committee. Determine the steering committee's scope and charter, as well as overall implementation issues, goals, and priorities. Make sure that the steering committee is trained to operate effectively as a team.

2. Select a facilitator. The facilitator may be chosen by the CEO when he organizes the steering committee, or choosing the facilitator may be one of the first steering committee activities.

3. Design the task force operating structure. Establish policies, procedures and roles. Draft a charter and create targets for task force work. Establish criteria for task force leaders and members.

4. Select people to serve on task forces and select task force leaders. Also, involve them in the process by asking that they finalize task force charters and targets. Also, ensure there is some formal mechanism for direct communication from the task force leaders to the CEO—the head of the steering committee. The task force head must believe he or she has direct access to the CEO so that problems and barriers to success surface quickly.

5. Along with task force leaders, map out a rough schedule of

major events. Develop and put in sequence the indoctrination, training, implementation, and communication plan.

6. Communicate the need, objectives, plan, performance expectations, and progress of each task force. Train task force leaders and teams. Monitor, motivate, and guide task force activities.

7. Continue the effort. Use the success of one task force's implementation project to develop more implementation projects. Where task forces make reports or recommendations, act on them.

The steering committee has primary responsibility for carrying out the steps after they are established. Membership on the steering committee may change over time. Determination of how and when this should occur is one of the activities of step 7.

STEERING COMMITTEE'S ROLE IN A JIT ENVIRONMENT

Operating in a JIT environment necessitates a structure where responsibility for problem solving and implementation of recommended plans is driven down into the organization. Operators, supervisors, individual contributors, and other staff personnel are assigned to task teams in order to solve operationally oriented problems.

Starting at this phase, the steering committee becomes the key component to the success of implementing the JIT program. Its consistent support reinforces the importance of JIT to the bottom line. This group has a variety of roles. Specialized orientation and training is almost always needed to prepare steering committee members to assume their roles and to complete their tasks. Emphasis should be placed on the following topics:

JIT project team planning

Principles of the management of planned change

Communication strategy

Team management

Problem solving

When we conduct such specialized training, the orientation session usually lasts one or two days and assists the steering committee to focus in and get organized around the task at hand. Because task teams will be undergoing a similar training process, there is a common language and shared experience between task teams and the steering committee. The success of JIT implementation can be tied to the steering committee's role in reviewing and implementing plans.

The steering committee must:

1. Select JIT problems to be solved.
2. Select team leaders.
3. Appoint a task force or task team to deal with each problem.
4. Ensure that progress meetings are held on a regular basis; monthly or more often as schedule or timetable warrants.
5. Provide guidance and coaching to teams. See to it that teams:

   Understand what their effort is all about and where it is heading.

   Are trained and skilled in problem solving.

   Select a recording secretary.
6. Regularly review the task teams' work.

   Assess accomplishments.

   Help solve problems.

   Resolve conflicts that teams or individuals encounter.

Disband task forces, reform them for new tasks.

7. Look at information needs under a JIT environment.

   What measures should be developed?

   How should reports be formatted?

   How frequent should reporting be?

   Where should reports be distributed?

   Who has responsibility for routine data gathering, summarization, and reporting?

7. Review reports to assess the progress of JIT and quality improvement, and determine and assign the next problems to be attacked.

8. Communicate progress, show encouragement, and generally act as the task team's champion.

9. Review recommendations from teams for remedial actions that require support or approval of higher management. Determine if such actions are justified and if so champion the cause.

WORKING WITHIN CONSTANT CHANGE

It is important to remember that steering committees are organic in nature and exist within the dynamic framework of a company. The group needs to continually make decisions based on changing information and even changing assumptions. There is a need to take action quickly where policies need changing.

Steering committees should try to determine priorities using two separate time lines and sets of criteria. One is the issue of where the company should be in three to five years, based on the vision and strategy created by senior management during the preparation phase. The other is a shorter-term, nine- to 12-month time line that gives people on task forces a realistic picture of what their goals ought to be. Success should be seen as meeting incremental goals, not merely reaching the ultimate goal.

Each steering committee must determine how the JIT implementation effort can be folded into the fabric of that particular company. Whether a company should institutionalize incremental gains rapidly or look for a few implementation successes before trying to set up measurements is one of the major questions the steering committee must answer at this point. The other is determining the priority of projects.

THE FACILITATOR

It is important that the steering committee have a staff person who works as the JIT day-to-day champion. This will often be a full-time job, or maybe a half-time job, with the same person working in the same capacity for the total quality steering committee if there is a TQ program going on simultaneously.

The individual assigned to this role needs to be trained in how to work as a resource to the JIT team. This person should be capable of working closely with task forces in the following ways:

1. Helping the JIT steering committee think in new and different ways necessary to the success of the JIT effort. This is often done by providing information on the successes and failures of other companies. This could mean setting up trips to see JIT at work in other companies, sponsoring people from other companies to address the steering committee, and ensuring a constant flow of reading material.

2. Understanding the implications of the JIT change effort and helping the steering committee understand its role.

3. Reinforcing the bottom-up aspect of JIT, while at the same time recognizing that JIT is also a top-down effort.

4. Counseling the task forces and particularly their leaders, subtly intervening in task force meetings to keep the work on track, and working one on one with task force members.

The role of JIT facilitator is a skilled one. It requires an individual who at minimum has an inclination not to seek the limelight, but is capable of being supportive to others and can develop good timing when making interventions and offering help.

Another role this person must play is to ensure that all the requisite capabilities necessary for JIT success are marshaled and aligned. Because of the cultural change aspect of JIT, the right training and organizational development capability is essential and the facilitator should look to the human resources department, or beyond, for such help.

TASK FORCES (TASK TEAMS)

Task forces, also called task teams or project teams, are focused teams designed and organized around specific problems. Each team brings specific skills and abilities that contribute to meeting specific objectives of the JIT implementation process. When an objective is reached, the team either ceases to exist or is reorganized to deal with another objective. JIT task forces work on solving problems or implementing specific procedures. Typically, these problems or procedures cut across departmental boundaries. The general process a task force should go through in doing this is:

Identify objectives

Establish what the group will and will not be responsible for

Set target date for implementation

Develop an action plan of steps to be taken

Analyze the impact of action steps on anticipated problems

Rank action steps

Identify people involved in or affected by each action step

Identify impact on current processes, procedures, and systems

Determine how to handle change

Develop communications procedures

MANAGEMENT OF TASK FORCES

The success of a task force's efforts depends on the way its activities are managed. Every task force has three key players:

The sponsor, either a particular executive or, more often in the case of JIT, the steering committee

The task force leader

Each member

Each has a specific and important role to play. In addition to these key players, other people in the organization can enhance or inhibit the likelihood of success for task forces. These include supervisors of task force members, those who have information or resources needed by the task force, and those who have a particular stake in the outcome of the task force's work.

One of the first tasks of the task force is to identify the stakeholders in its work and to develop a plan to get their constructive involvement in the project.

TASK FORCE LEADER

A task force leader is both a project manager and a group facilitator.

The project manager is called upon to plan and organize the group's meetings and other activities, to oversee task implementation, to ensure that records are kept of actions and decisions, and to coordinate all communications about the task force's work. This aspect of the job will be handled more efficiently and effectively if the team leader makes full use of the group's individual and collective resources in carrying out this charge. That means that being responsible does not necessarily mean doing it oneself.

This is where the team leader's other role, that of group facilitator, becomes critical. As group facilitator, the team leader's job is to coordinate the efforts of individual members, to facilitate or make easier their ability to work together as a team. Part of this job involves encouraging other group members to participate fully and to take on leadership roles throughout the course of the project. The more effective a leader becomes as a group facilitator, the easier the project manager task becomes.

Some companies have dedicated one team leader to as many as four or five teams, effectively making a team leader a full-time position. The most common practice, however, is to give a team leader only one or two teams to work with. This keeps team leaders from burning out on special projects. The equivalent of one full day a week is devoted to working for each team—about two hours for each team's meeting and another six hours each week to get things done from meeting to meeting.

GENERAL GUIDELINES

Some general guidelines for task forces include:

1. *Group Size.* As groups get larger, flexibility and effectiveness are reduced. Each task force should have 5 to 10 people.
2. *Membership.* Members should come from all areas and functions involved in the change to be implemented. In most cases, a majority of the task force should be made up of shop-floor employees rather than white collar employees.
3. *Scheduling.* Groups should meet at least once every two weeks, and more often at the beginning of their work. The

time of the meetings should be consistent and predetermined so everyone can put the meetings on their calendars and incorporate them into their regular schedules. Meetings should be limited to one or two hours in general.

4. *Duration.*   Task forces are temporary and goal oriented. When the task force's goals are reached, it should be disbanded or reconstituted for another task. Task forces should usually be in existence for less than one year, and many only last three to six months.

5. *Accountability.*   Each member should realize that effort and sacrifice are necessary. Consistent attendance at meetings is necessary, as is a willingness to take on assignments within the action plan.

6. *Documentation.*   Meetings should follow written agendas, and minutes should be taken for later distribution, both within the task force and to the facilitator and the steering committee. Progress reports should be written and any recommendations for future action should take the form of written reports or memos.

MAKING THE TEAM WORK

In order to make the team function effectively, there must be some basic training in teamwork for all team members and leadership training for leaders. Part of that training should be in the area of structured problem solving, a set of steps used to solve problems. These sessions should also deal with topics such as interpersonal skills, meeting management, influence and negotiating skills, and the impact of different learning styles on problem solving and teamwork. For implementation of JIT, team members also need technical training in specific JIT techniques.

The steering committee must design a basic team charter, then modify that to create specific charters for each task force. The objectives of each task force must be defined and expressed in a way that can be measured. The scope of the task force's actions must be outlined, as must the life of the task force and how it will be operated.

A task force without a clear charter, boundaries, and performance expectations will spend much of its time making guesses about what the steering committee wants, how it is expected to achieve these objectives, and on what basis the task force's performance will ultimately be measured.

On the other hand, too narrow or rigid an initial definition of its territory may leave task force members with little potential for a creative approach to the task. It is therefore important for the steering committee to carefully do the following before task forces are created:

1. Think through the potential project areas for task force assignment. Which ones represent the richest territories for exploration by a task force? In the case of creating a JIT environment, think through which product lines would benefit most by reducing setup times and having smaller product runs, which would benefit most by machine cells, and which would benefit most by instituting pull systems. Think through which opportunities have:

   Most pressing need

   Highest potential ROI

   Best learning opportunity

   Most support available

2. Think through a general charter statement for each task force to be established. Specifically, what should the task force hope to accomplish?

3. Define the parameters, performance expectations, and resources within which the task force is expected to operate. Consider such issues as:

   Full- or part-time participation of members

   Scope of the project

When the task should be completed

Budget

Application of training resources

What information will and will not be available to the team

How much decision-making authority the team has

Who needs to be communicated with

What performance benchmarks are being looked for

What a successful task force product would look like

4. Think through the qualities needed in task force leaders.

5. Think through the qualities needed in task force members.

While these activities will not guarantee success, they increase the likelihood that the task force leader and members will be able to carry out their mission with the least amount of wasted time and effort, and with the confidence that comes from a clear understanding of the steering committee's expectations.

FEATURES AND BENEFITS OF TASK FORCES

Task forces can serve as powerful management tools capable of accomplishing many simultaneous objectives. Some of the benefits are:

Attention is focused on the importance of the issues the task force addresses.

Resources can be temporarily concentrated to resolve an issue without disrupting day-to-day activities.

The right people with the right skills and knowledge are brought together in a focused effort.

A variety of groups can be represented through task force

membership, including those whose commitment and support will be required for successful implementation.

Concerns and objections can be handled as constructive input before decisions are reached, resulting in higher quality solutions and increased likelihood of final acceptance.

Top management can demonstrate its commitment to teamwork through support of task force efforts.

Decision making can be pushed deeper into the organization.

As with anything, the strengths of task forces have within them the seeds of possible difficulties. A task force must be properly managed by both the task force leader and the steering committee if it is to avoid some common pitfalls:

1. Individual task force members from different parts of the organization bring with them a diversity of viewpoints, goals, and loyalties that could make the task force a battleground for fighting out long-standing departmental conflicts. They also bring different learning styles, different ways to approach problems, and different ways to make decisions.

2. The temporary nature of the task force and the fact that it parallels other ongoing responsibilities may limit members' willingness to commit personal time and energy to the project. This is especially true if members' immediate supervisors have not indicated clear support for the task force members' participation.

3. Private agendas get in the way, especially those of ambitious managers looking to score points with senior management.

4. The creation of a task force is seen by many nonmembers as a criticism of current practices and programs. This can lead to tensions between members and nonmembers.

These pitfalls can be avoided if the task force process is appropriately planned, communicated, and managed by the steering committee, and if it has the full support of senior management.

One final note should be made about organizations.

There is a danger in using a special organization to implement Just In Time. While the steering committee/task force model is effective and has been proven to produce results, it carries with it a risk that a subtle message will be sent to the line organization that JIT is the responsibility of the steering committee and the task forces.

There is a practical limit to how many people can be involved in the early stages of JIT and therefore the danger that those not directly involved will not embrace the philosophy and not recognize its benefits. This is a danger that the JIT facilitator must avoid through constantly providing information for those who are not involved in the day-to-day workings of implementing JIT, and by making sure that those who are involved do some of this communicating. The organization must be aware of what steps are being taken, why, and what the results of those steps are. The top managers must also make sure that widespread participation in the JIT implementation effort takes place as early in that effort as possible.

13

PUTTING THE PLAN
INTO ACTION

Now that a vision and strategy for the company have been established and the proper organization has been put in place to turn that vision and strategy into reality, it is time to begin implementing pilot projects. Then, using what is learned from the pilot projects, a company must determine exactly what measurement systems need to be kept, modified, or created in order to operate in the new JIT environment and institutionalize the new manufacturing philosophy.

Because JIT is antithetical to so much of the ingrained Western manufacturing approach, there is great potential for resistance—partly to the technical aspects of JIT, but even more to the social implications of those technical changes. Employees must become familiar with the technical changes, and understand the reasons for and the social implications of these changes. Pilots are a good way to do this in a nonthreatening way, when the stakes are not as great as they would be if the entire manufacturing process were being changed all at once. After pilots have been successfully run, it is important to continue the implementation of JIT on a project-by-project basis.

Resistance to change is not something that can usually be dealt with merely through logic. Overcoming resistance to change is often more like a biological process. I like to use Joseph Juran's analogy of chickens hatching. It takes the same number of days today for chicks to hatch as it took thousands of years ago. No matter what chicken farmers do they cannot speed that process up. If they apply heat to an egg to try to get it to hatch faster, all they get is a hard-boiled egg.

It is the same with people learning a new way of doing things. If heat is applied to the workers on the shop floor, all that happens is hard-boiled employees.

Pilot projects are necessary to get people to make changes. Pilots provide employees with a number of opportunities. Employees are able to learn a new game in a limited, controlled way. Pilot projects give employees time to integrate JIT ideas, see something physical, and deal with specific worries and objections one at a time.

Although it is possible to give general guidelines, each company must make a number of decisions on how it can best go through the process.

In general, though, it is safe to say that pilots should be done slowly, taking care to work through them fully before expanding throughout the entire manufacturing process. Also, generally, it is usually better to have some successful pilots before beginning the education process throughout the entire company. Some companies try to do mass training on all the different aspects of JIT at the beginning of their implementation process. Unfortunately, this often has the disadvantage of getting employees excited about a new concept, but not providing them with any concrete results to see, often leading them to the feeling that JIT is just one more of management's projects of the month.

HOW AND WHY TO CHOOSE PILOTS

Choosing pilot projects and the people to work on those projects is one of the most sensitive aspects of planning a JIT program. The purpose of any pilot is 50 percent for the learning experience and only 50 percent to achieve impressive, measurable results.

Results don't have to be impressive in terms of dollars. It is enough to be impressive in terms of percentage gains. Solving a small problem in a controlled environment could yield gains of up to 15 to 30 percent in terms of direct labor, 90 percent in terms of inventory, and 90 percent in terms of throughput. The dollars may only be a few thousand, but the example will show people that the same thing can happen in other, more significant areas.

Some general rules of thumb for picking pilots are:

1. Choose pilots based on the people involved. The best people usually will get the best results. Remember, JIT pilots set the tone for the entire JIT effort. Pilots should be picked based on the highest probability for success. *JIT projects simply cannot be allowed to fail.* When it is not possible to get the best of both worlds—the best project and the best people—I recommend going with the best people. The ideal person for a JIT pilot will be progressive, aggressive, creative, energetic, and, above all, respected by his or her peers.

2. Do not pick a pilot where a large, chronic problem must be solved. The problem should be big enough so that solving it will matter, but not the biggest problem in the system, or one that has long frustrated people who have tried to solve it in the past.

3. Do not pick a pilot where the process is not predictable. The process should be under control in terms of both product quality and equipment reliability.

4. Do not pick a pilot where there is a bottleneck. There should be ample capacity so that there is freedom to stop the process, analyze possible solutions to a problem, experiment with those possible solutions, and still produce enough to meet customer needs. There needs to be enough capacity to be able to make a mistake and recover from it.

INSTITUTIONALIZATION

Institutionalizing the gains of JIT is really changing the climate of the company. This needs to be done in a well thought out, consistent, and calm manner.

After a number of pilots have been run, it is time to use these successes as levers to change the manufacturing philosophy throughout the company. Changing the manufacturing philosophy means changing the way manufacturing success is defined and measured, first by changing the definitions in people's minds, then by changing the measurement systems in all their forms.

In some ways, institutionalizing JIT should have been going on from the very beginning of the implementation process, when senior management started putting out messages that JIT is the direction the company should be going in. Before pilots were even undertaken, senior management should have let it be known that the rules of the game were going to be different under JIT, that the company's manufacturing philosophy would change.

Existing management tools should be used to make the change to a JIT environment, rather than brass bands and other fanfare. Regular plant communications (such as newsletters, newspapers, and bulletin boards) should be used to keep all employees apprised of where in the JIT implementation plan the company is. The regular departmental monthly or quarterly reviews should be used to explain and emphasize changes in measurement systems. At each of these reviews, management must be visible and must ask a consistent set of questions about how the pilot effort is going and how employees are reacting to it. Management should not underestimate the power of constant and consistent questioning to keep JIT on track and keep employees' interest in JIT at a peak. Face-to-face questioning is a far more powerful form of communication than memos. New objectives, expectations, and measurements should be initiated at a natural time—usually the next budgeting period.

It needs to be made clear to pilot project team members that they will be conducting their project under a special set of circumstances—a transitional stage. Although the new rules will not apply—in fact there probably will not be any new rules in existence—the old rules will not apply, either.

Management should not send out such measurements as typical cost-accounting reports. Some companies make the mistake of telling pilot project teams that regular reports will be sent out but to disregard them. This won't work. The reports must be suspended for the duration of the pilot.

Union contracts are as much institutions as company systems—unions should be encouraged to participate in the process by agreeing to the suspension of work practices for the duration of pilots—practices such as incentive pay, bumping, and narrow job descriptions. Management's part in this is to make sure that no one loses money or rights during this period.

During the period of a pilot, all members of the pilot team should be encouraged to suggest ways in which the new environment should be measured. New rules do not have to be set up immediately, but it should be recognized that many rules will change.

The most common areas where measurement systems need to be changed are:

1. Machine utilization

2. Direct and indirect labor ratios

3. Overhead ratios

4. Measuring speed

5. Setup and run times

6. Cost per purchase order

7. Standard costing

Machine Utilization

The only time this is a valid measurement in a JIT environment is as a measure of capacity when a company is trying to decide whether or not to buy more equipment. In actual practice, the way this measurement is used now is not as a measure of capacity, rather it becomes a message sent to the shop floor that idle equipment is bad. It causes supervisors to use equipment whether product is needed or not.

Direct and Indirect Labor Ratios

This measurement is particularly troublesome under JIT. Its proper use is to keep direct and indirect labor in proper relation in times when volumes are changing but methods are staying the same. It is therefore not appropriate to use when methods change. In fact, it will cause resistance to any methods change, including automation, that would reduce direct labor more than it would reduce indirect labor.

This measurement sends out a general message that direct labor is good and indirect labor is bad. The real message of JIT is that cost is cost.

Too often I have seen middle managers reject legitimate measures that cut direct-labor costs because the measurement system penalizes them for eliminating direct labor by insisting on a concurrent reduction in indirect labor.

Overhead Ratios

By using overhead ratios a company sends the message that not only indirect labor, but overhead, is bad, and that direct labor is good. There is a traditional cost-accounting belief that direct labor is measurable and identifiable, but that indirect labor and overhead are not identifiable and therefore can get out of control easily, so they should be pegged to the level of direct labor. If direct labor is up, the theory goes, volume must be up, but if indirect labor or overhead go up, things must be getting sloppy.

If a JIT program reduces both labor and material costs, that hurts the overhead ratio. A company can reduce total cost and look bad. For instance, if the typical cost breakdown for a $10 item is:

$ 7	Material
1	Labor
2	Overhead
$10	

the overhead is 20 percent. If, after implementation of a successful JIT program, the cost has decreased to $7.50 and the breakdown is:

$5	Material
0.50	Labor
2	Overhead
$7.50	

the overhead is 27 percent. The item's cost has decreased 25 percent, but the percentage of total cost that is overhead has increased by about 33 percent.

This message—that despite cutting costs the person who allows overhead to increase as a percentage of total cost is a bad guy—causes much resistance to JIT.

Japanese companies and progressive Western companies have much more willingness to make global measurements of results—total input to total output. As long as the results are good and getting better, there is no need to micro measure.

Hewlett Packard is experimenting with eliminating entirely the separate measurements of direct and indirect labor. What does it matter? is the argument; a payroll hour is a payroll hour.

Measuring Speed

One of the most common ways to express standards, both in terms of measuring performance and even paying people, is in pieces per hour. This is a measurement of speed. But in a JIT environment companies are no longer trying to produce as fast as possible, but instead to produce enough to meet customer requirements. What makes sense in this environment is to measure variable cost per price. Instead of a part being produced at a speed of x per hour, it is produced at a cost of y hours of direct labor per 100 parts. Speed can always be changed, as long as the ratio of cost/production is maintained.

Setup and Run Times

Having ratios of setup to run time sends a message that run time is good and setup time is bad. Wherever setups can be avoided or made more quickly, this measurement will cause people to either produce more whether it is needed or not, or to idle machinery. In either case, the ratio will improve. This ratio will resist the JIT requirement that reduced setup times be reinvested into more frequent setups and reduced lot sizes.

Cost Per Purchase Order

Again, this measurement had an original purpose of controlling changes in volume on the assumption that methods stay the same. The cost-per-purchase-order measurement says blanket orders and systems contracting are bad, because the cost per order goes up. But if the goal is eliminating paperwork—a waste—blanket orders and systems contracting are a wonderful tool.

Under JIT, the cost per purchase order will necessarily rise, since one of the goals of JIT purchasing is to reduce the number of purchase orders necessary to procure a given amount of material.

Standard Costing

Companies are just beginning to see the pitfalls of standard costing. If it is used to decide what equipment a company should purchase, it can definitely lead to the wrong decision. This is because standard cost only measures how much it costs to make a product when a piece of equipment is running as fast as it can.

For example, a client of ours needed to buy a new glass furnace to produce a specialty item. The company had a choice between a furnace that had an 80-pound capacity or one that had a 400-pound capacity.

The 80-pound furnace cost less to run, cost less to purchase, and used fewer people. There would be less glass lost during changeover from one product to another, and the 80-pound capacity was enough to produce the amount of product required. All the evidence told the company to buy the smaller furnace. But standard costing said buy the bigger furnace.

In this case some of the basic assumptions of standard costing threw the calculations off. First is the assumption that the machine will always be busy and that people will always be there to run the machine. In this type of situation, neither of those assumptions is true.

If the 80-pound capacity furnace is big enough, the 400-pound capacity furnace will be idle 80 percent of the time.

Because of the assumption that the machine will always be used, depreciation is handled wrong. Depreciation is put into a general overhead account and spread over 12 months. If the depreciation of a 400-pound furnace is calculated on the 20 percent of the time it would actually be in use, the true cost would be seen to be much higher.

In addition, because of the assumption that people would always be there, standard costing cannot account for other costs, such as training and layoff costs, caused by the fact that people are needed only 20 percent of the time.

AN ALTERNATIVE

These are seven examples of measurements that are either incorrect, used incorrectly, or simply not applicable in a JIT environment. A totally new system of measurement and reward is necessary.

A type of measurement and reward system we have found to work well in a JIT environment is gain sharing. A description of gain sharing should serve as a model for what kinds of measurements should be incorporated into a successful JIT environment.

Gain sharing plans are becoming more popular because they reward people for doing things that reduce the total labor cost and, in some plans, the material cost of a product. Gain sharing plans encourage people to work together because gains in productivity are shared equally among all the people covered by the plan.

The cost savings of productivity gains have traditionally belonged to the business or management. Sharing means that the savings that would normally accrue to the company will be less than if the gains were not shared, but that those gains will be spread across a larger base of people in the organization.

Companies that decide to share gains must promote a climate that encourages people to work together. The problem is that many companies do not know how to promote such a climate. This is particularly true in companies that replace traditional wage incentive plans or piecework plans with gain sharing plans.

Gain sharing is especially applicable to a JIT environment. In gain sharing, a current standard of performance is developed by identifying how many total payroll hours are needed to provide a current product.

Gains are calculated by taking net sales (sales minus returns) and calculating the number of standard payroll hours represented and comparing that to actual payroll hours during the period. As the company learns to use less actual payroll hours for a given amount of sales, gains occur, which are shared—usually equally—between the company and the part of the work force that is covered by the gain sharing plan.

Gain sharing is not profit sharing. Profit sharing requires opening up the company books and sharing the total profit. Gain sharing starts at today's position by calculating a current standard and sharing only those gains made in the future.

Gain sharing differs from traditional measurements in many ways—all of them appropriate within a JIT environment. There are two overriding aspects to gain sharing. One is that gain sharing is a global measurement—measuring total input for total output and focusing only on bottom-line gains. Isolated efficiencies such as increased speeds are no longer rewarded unless they contribute to a reduction of total cost. The second is sharing of the gains with all employees. This involves all employees and promotes teamwork rather than individual performance. Some specific ways gain sharing changes traditional measurements are that it:

Rewards reducing total cost, not just specific costs

Rewards making only what is needed, not making as much as possible

Rewards getting costs out, rather than getting up speed of production

Rewards doing it right the first time and finding permanent solutions to problems, because doing it right the first time has to require fewer hours than doing it over again

Rewards eliminating activities rather than protecting jobs

Rewards reducing inventories, because a reduction in inventory means a company sells something and doesn't spend payroll hours to replace it. Conversely, there is a penalty for producing something that does not get sold in the same period.

It should be obvious that gain sharing helps foster an atmosphere conducive to successful implementation of JIT, an atmosphere where the JIT goals—balance, doing it right the first time, and continuous improvement—can be paramount.

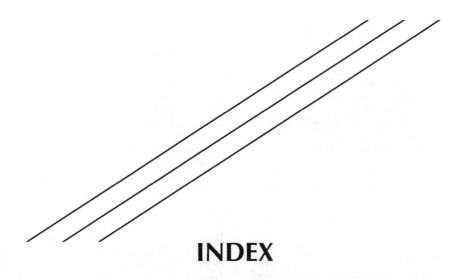

INDEX

219